JUMPSTART
TALK FOR LEARNING

Jumpstart! Talk for Learning presents a collection of multi-sensory games and activities that will jumpstart children's use of effective talk in the classroom. This book offers practical and engaging ideas ranging from brief games to extended lesson suggestions. It offers a basis for creating your own spoken language activities to match the topics you are teaching and the individual needs of your class.

Specifically written to help teachers with the direct teaching of talk skills required by the National Curriculum, activities in the book encourage children to:

- participate in group and class discussions
- use exploratory talk and share a range of points of view
- use talk imaginatively to develop understanding
- develop individual presentational talk
- take part in active drama sessions.

Jumpstart! Talk for Learning includes a range of classroom activities that can be used in literacy lessons and integrated across the curriculum. This essential resource will help teachers develop children's use of talk to understand one another and get things done together.

Lyn Dawes is a consultant in Spoken Language in the Primary Years, previously Senior Lecturer in Education at the University of Northampton, UK and visiting lecturer at the University of Cambridge, UK.

John Foster taught English for 20 years before becoming a full-time writer. He has written over 100 books for classroom use and is a highly regarded children's poet.

Jumpstart!

Jumpstart! Grammar (2nd Edition)
Games and activities for ages 7–14
Pie Corbett and Julia Strong

Jumpstart! Talk for Learning
Games and activities for ages 7–12
Lyn Dawes and John Foster

Jumpstart! PSHE
Games and activities for ages 7–13
John Foster

Jumpstart! History
Engaging activities for ages 7–12
*Sarah Whitehouse and
Karen Vickers-Hulse*

Jumpstart! Geography
Engaging activities for ages 7–12
Sarah Whitehouse and Mark Jones

Jumpstart! Thinking Skills and Problem Solving
Games and activities for ages 7–14
Steve Bowkett

Jumpstart! Maths (2nd Edition)
Maths activities and games for ages 5–14
John Taylor

Jumpstart! Spanish and Italian
Engaging activities for ages 7–12
Catherine Watts and Hilary Phillips

Jumpstart! French and German
Engaging activities for ages 7–12
Catherine Watts and Hilary Phillips

Jumpstart! Drama
Games and activities for ages 5–11
*Teresa Cremin, Roger McDonald,
Emma Goff and Louise Blakemore*

Jumpstart! Science
Games and activities for ages 5–11
Rosemary Feasey

Jumpstart! Storymaking
Games and activities for ages 7–12
Pie Corbett

Jumpstart! Poetry
Games and activities for ages 7–12
Pie Corbett

Jumpstart! Creativity
Games and activities for ages 7–14
Steve Bowkett

Jumpstart! ICT
ICT activities and games for ages 7–14
John Taylor

Jumpstart! Numeracy
Maths activities and games for ages 5–14
John Taylor

Jumpstart! Literacy
Key Stage 2/3 literacy games
Pie Corbett

JUMPSTART!
TALK FOR LEARNING

GAMES AND ACTIVITIES FOR AGES 7–12

Lyn Dawes and John Foster

LONDON AND NEW YORK

First published 2016
by Routledge
2 Park Square, Milton Park, Abingdon, Oxon OX14 4RN

and by Routledge
711 Third Avenue, New York, NY 10017

Routledge is an imprint of the Taylor & Francis Group, an informa business

© 2016 Lyn Dawes and John Foster

The right of Lyn Dawes and John Foster to be identified as authors of this work has been asserted by them in accordance with sections 77 and 78 of the Copyright, Designs and Patents Act 1988.

All rights reserved. No part of this book may be reprinted or reproduced or utilised in any form or by any electronic, mechanical, or other means, now known or hereafter invented, including photocopying and recording, or in any information storage or retrieval system, without permission in writing from the publishers.

Trademark notice: Product or corporate names may be trademarks or registered trademarks, and are used only for identification and explanation without intent to infringe.

British Library Cataloguing in Publication Data
A catalogue record for this book is available from the British Library

Library of Congress Cataloging in Publication Data
Names: Dawes, Lyn, author. | Foster, John, 1941 October 12- author.
Title: Jumpstart! talk for learning : games and activities for ages 7-12 / Lyn Dawes and John Foster.
Description: Abingdon, Oxon ; New York, NY : Routledge, 2016.
Identifiers: LCCN 2015023431 | ISBN 9781138899261 (hbk) | ISBN 9781138899278 (pbk) | ISBN 9781315708003 (ebk)
Subjects: LCSH: Language arts (Elementary)--Activity programs. | Educational games.
Classification: LCC LB1576 .D239 2016 | DDC 372.6--dc23LC record available at http://lccn.loc.gov/2015023431

ISBN: 978-1-138-89926-1 (hbk)
ISBN: 978-1-138-89927-8 (pbk)
ISBN: 978-1-315-70800-3 (ebk)

Typeset in Palatino and Scala Sans
by Saxon Graphics Ltd, Derby

This book is dedicated to:

Mrs Steele, Mrs Arkle and the staff and children at
Cosgrove Village Primary School, Northamptonshire

Contents

The power of talk	ix
Preface	xi
Acknowledgements	xiii
Introduction	xv

PART 1
Learning through talk   1

1 **Talking and learning**   3
   Raising awareness of the importance of talk   5
   Teaching exploratory talk skills   8
   Talk for Learning in science: habitats   9
   Creating class Ground Rules for Talk   14

2 **Listening and learning**   16
   Raising awareness of particular listening skills   16
   Listening activities   18
   Feedback and the importance of listening   23

3 **Assessment and progression**   24
   Assessment questions for a range of types of talk   27
   Assessing group discussion skills   34
   Auditing a child's discussion skills   35
   Assessing specialised talk   36
   Progression in talk skills   37
   Summary   40

Contents

PART 2
Curriculum activities and games   41

4 Opinions, argument and persuasion   43
   Opinions and points of view   43
   Developing an argument   52
   Persuading and debating   67

5 Conveying information   77
   Describing   78
   Recounting   82
   Reporting   87
   Explaining   92
   Instructing   94

6 Talk across the curriculum   101
   Paired Learning Intentions   101
   Special opportunities for talk across the curriculum   105
   Ideas for cross-curricular talk   110
   Taking roles in a group   114

7 Talk about stories, poems and drama   118
   Talk about stories   118
   Talk about poems   128
   Talk about drama and improvisation   142

8 Summary and resources   146
   The importance of talk   146
   Other resources   148

The power of talk

'What do you think?' said the girl.
'I'm not sure,' said the boy.
'Neither am I,' said the girl.
'Let's talk about it,' said the boy.

So the girl spoke and the boy listened
And the boy spoke and the girl listened.
Thoughts flew between them.
Ideas bubbled to the surface.

Opinions clashed
As they wrestled with words,
They exchanged arguments,
And sought reasons.

Sometimes they fell silent.
Then a light would flash
Illuminating a new pathway
For them to explore.

Eventually, the girl said,
'I think I know what I think.'
'I think I do too,' said the boy
And they agreed to disagree.

John Foster

Preface

It is widely recognised that children's ability to use spoken language can affect their educational progress. And yet the teaching of talk skills is rarely given the priority it deserves in Primary classrooms. Developing children's confidence and skills as speakers can assist their learning, as well as enabling their wider participation in society. The National Primary Curriculum for England and Wales reflects this when it states that all pupils should be taught how to use spoken language effectively.

Teachers have the professional expertise to create classroom environments where children confidently express their views and where they will listen thoughtfully to the teacher and to the contributions of others. I am sure that primary teachers will welcome this book, which provides such excellent resources for developing children's talk skills in the classroom – and which does so in ways that ensure that children will enjoy participating in activities as they learn.

Neil Mercer
University of Cambridge

Acknowledgements

The authors would like to acknowledge the invaluable help given by family and friends in writing and editing this book. In particular we would like to thank Bruce Roberts at Routledge and hope he can find us next time we meet up at the Grand Café in Oxford.

We are grateful to these schools and teachers for their generous contributions:

- Orchard School, East Molesey, Surrey; Carol, Jess and Chloe
- Eastwood School, Bradford; Jan Carrier
- Greenlane School, Bradford; Jane Townend
- Carol Satterthwaite, Primary Literacy Consultant and champion of effective talk in classrooms, http://www.carolsatterthwaite.com
- Independent booksellers Roving Books for their help and encouragement, http://www.rovingbooks.com.

Lyn Dawes and John Foster,
June 2015

Introduction

> With an understanding that communication skills are the key indicator of future success, it is clearly imperative to have a 'Talking Classroom' in a 'Talking School'.
>
> KS2 teacher

> High quality classroom dialogue and the teaching of language structures which underpin [communication skills] are essential to high quality classroom learning.
>
> KS2 teacher

This book is about the hugely important subject of children's spoken language use in the classroom. Children usually arrive in our classrooms able to speak. But they may not know what sort of talk can best help them learn, and help their classmates learn. They need direct teaching of the talk skills which will ensure that talk in the classroom fosters learning; and they need to be aware that the quality of their talk with others matters.

Teachers have the responsibility for organising and planning children's use of spoken language – talk – during their time in class; it is part of our job to decide who speaks, and when. Teachers demonstrate how to talk in ways that help everyone to learn and, in doing so, act as a model for talk, with children learning by example how to listen, reason, explain and consider ideas. Teachers also offer children crucially important examples of how to discuss and reflect aloud on a range of points of view.

An essential element of 'becoming an educated person' is learning how to listen and to talk to others, to solve problems and see other points of view in discussion; to get things done through talk. And so an understanding of how and why to talk in this way is what we need to teach. Teaching of the most useful talk skills involves developing a child's capacity to articulate both tentative and more firmly held ideas. Children in talk-focused classrooms can learn to express themselves clearly and with confidence, and have the skills to listen to others and evaluate what they hear. For some children, the classroom is their best chance to speak, listen, think and learn in systematic ways which will stick with them always; indeed, for a few, the classroom is their only hope of ever really thinking aloud and finding their voice. For all children, the classroom can be a terrific forum for the sharing of ideas and understanding with their peers, a collaborative hot-house of expanding minds.

Jumpstart! Talk for Learning provides a theory-based approach to teaching spoken language structures to equip children with the necessary skills. Its aim is to support teachers who wish to elicit children's ideas, to enable children to express themselves with confidence, and to create a classroom in which 'knowing more' or 'knowing better' than others is not the aim; instead, children learn how to share and build on their knowledge, ensuring both individual and joint achievement. They learn how to respect what others say, and how to provide positive and useful oral feedback. The book will to help you to teach children how to hold their own in a rational discussion, tackling ideas rather than taking issue with one another personally, and learning the talk tools which will equip them to challenge, negotiate and ultimately come to an understanding about problems.

All this involves a range of talk skills which are interlinked, very teachable and yet may never be mentioned in class, let alone formally taught. In essence we need to teach children how to talk effectively to one another about their learning. We know that quietness can be conducive to learning, and that noisy chatter can prevent learning. But we are happily past the days of children seated in silent rows. We are also long past the type of loose 'group work' in which children shared a table and worked on similar things, but in which competition defeated co-operation, and children got on with their individual tasks, with talk kept to a minimum. We know that classrooms should not be monumentally silent, and similarly we know that as off-task talk begins, learning falls away. There is fortunately a happy medium for group work in which talk is general, but clearly focused on the task in hand; in which the structures of discussion and debate are learned and practised to everyone's advantage, and put to use in an everyday way. The activities in this book can help to establish a classroom in which children are taught about the power of talk, and in which an awareness of talk for learning leads children to recognise their role in thinking for themselves, and developing the thinking of their classmates.

Grouping for talk

Different talk activities require different kinds of grouping. There are many ways to organise learning groups. In this book we use these groups:

1 **Friendship groups** – membership is your choice or the children's; this grouping is for collaborative, creative and cumulative tasks in which children need to feel relaxed and easy with one another, in order to pursue personal goals, undertake projects and provide a context for self-motivated learning.

2 **Exploratory groups** – membership is your choice; this grouping is for exploratory talk between firmly established discussion groups of three, of mixed ability, in which there is a range of opinion and interests, offering the chance to hear and consider different points of view.

Exploratory groups can be re-combined or altered to include others from different groups, so that children experience further chances to explain, persuade and negotiate and to hear a wider range of points of view.

3 **Ability groups** – membership is your choice; this grouping helps children to work on specific aspects of the curriculum alongside children doing likewise. Ability groups are always open to review as children develop. Since work is usually individual, there may be little needed in the way of discussion skills.

4 **Talk pairs** – younger children, or children learning English as an additional language, may need to start their talk work with just one other child. This helps them to focus on and develop a particular talk or listening skill, or to think about turn-taking and so on, without having to cope with too great a diversity of ideas.

TALK FOR LEARNING IN THE NATIONAL CURRICULUM

The National Curriculum includes statutory requirements for the teaching and learning of Spoken language for Years 1–6. Spoken language development therefore must be included in your planning. The National Curriculum statements provide an entitlement for every child and the teacher can feel confident in offering **direct teaching** of spoken language.

Spoken language – talk – of course needs a context, and in this *Jumpstart!* book we have provided a range of games, activities and suggestions which you can use and re-purpose to teach the full range of the curriculum.

This section provides detail on the National Curriculum requirements; it suggests a set of **Learning Intentions** for the **direct teaching of talk**, and practice in the sort of talk specified. To match these and consolidate learning, we also provide **Plenary Discussion** suggestions which you can use to bring out important points about children's developing use of talk in every session.

Our suggestion is that your curriculum lessons should have a parallel 'Talk for Learning' component as often as possible, so that the talk that goes on is regular, purposeful and focused. Such everyday use of talk can help the child to learn and practise talk skills, at the same time as helping them to learn to discuss subjects such as science, literature or mathematics using appropriate vocabulary.

The National Curriculum offers a wonderfully extensive range of contexts through which children can learn the language structures and skills to talk about their developing thinking. Here are the Primary National Curriculum statements related to talk.

The National Curriculum statutory requirements for spoken language

Pupils should be taught to:

1 listen and respond appropriately to adults and their peers

2 ask relevant questions to extend their understanding and knowledge

3 use relevant strategies to build their vocabulary

4 articulate and justify answers, arguments and opinions

5 give well-structured descriptions, explanations and narratives for different purposes, including for expressing feelings

6 maintain attention and participate actively in collaborative conversations, staying on topic and initiating and responding to comments

7 use spoken language to develop understanding through speculating, hypothesising, imagining and exploring ideas

8 speak audibly and fluently with an increasing command of Standard English

9 participate in discussions, presentations, performances, role play, improvisations and debates

10 gain, maintain and monitor the interest of the listener(s)

11 consider and evaluate different viewpoints, attending to and building on the contributions of others

12 select and use appropriate registers for effective communication.

Introduction

TALK FOR LEARNING: LEARNING INTENTIONS AND PLENARY DISCUSSIONS

This section takes each of the National Curriculum statements in the list and suggests talk Learning Intentions (LIs) and ideas for Plenary Discussions (PDs) which you can **pair up with your curriculum LIs and PDs**. In this way the all-important Talk for Learning becomes integrated into everyday classroom life.

1 **Listen and respond appropriately to adults and their peers**

   LI: To *listen* and show you have listened by *replying*.

   PD: Who listened to you? How could you tell?
   Who did you listen to; what did they say? How did you reply?
   What did you learn by listening?
   Why is listening sometimes difficult?
   What makes it easier to listen?

2 **Ask relevant questions to extend their understanding and knowledge**

   LI: To ask a question.

   PD: Who asked you a question? Could you answer it?
   Who did you ask to tell you something? Was their answer clear?
   When are questions useful?
   What did you learn by asking a question? Who did you learn from?

3 **Use relevant strategies to build their vocabulary**

   LI: To *use a new word*.

   PD: Who did you talk to about (*new word*)?
   Can you and your partner explain what it means?
   Can you say how or when you could use this word at home?

4 **Articulate and justify answers, arguments and opinions**

   LI: To *give a reason for what you say.*
         To *use the word 'because' in your answer.*

   PD: Who gave you a reason for their idea?
         Was it an interesting reason?
         Did you discuss different reasons?
         Who heard a reason that helped you to learn or change your mind?

5 **Give well-structured descriptions, explanations and narratives for different purposes, including for expressing feelings**

   LI: To *explain* how you feel.

   PD: Can anyone give an example of a clear explanation they've heard today?
         Can you say how someone else feels about this?
         Can you tell us someone who is good at giving explanations?
         What do they do or say that is helpful when explaining?

6 **Maintain attention and participate actively in collaborative conversations, staying on topic and initiating and responding to comments**

   LI: To *concentrate* on (stick to) the topic we are working on.

   PD: Who helped you concentrate on the topic?
         Who asked you to join in or share your ideas?
         Who have you learned from by listening to what they said?

7 **Use spoken language to develop understanding through speculating, hypothesising, imagining and exploring ideas**

   LI: To use the *question 'What if…?'*

   PD: Who asked a 'What if…?' question? How did you answer it?

What did you hear that made you think harder?
Whose ideas did you like? Why?

8 **Speak audibly and fluently with an increasing command of Standard English**

LI: To *speak aloud* about our topic to the whole class.

PD: Comment *favourably* on the oral presentations *(which may be one sentence)*.

9 **Participate in discussions, presentations, performances, role play, improvisations and debates**

LI: To join in with the discussion so that everyone contributes.

PD: Who encouraged you to join in?
What was good about your group talk?
What did you get done by talking together?
Who would you say is a good group member and why?

10 **Gain, maintain and monitor the interest of the listener(s)**

LI: To *encourage people to listen to you.*

PD: What strategies do we use to gain attention?
Who did you think was interesting to listen to? Why?
Can you say how you encourage people to listen to you at home?

11 **Consider and evaluate different viewpoints, attending to and building on the contributions of others**

LI: To *chain ideas together.*

PD: Can you give a summary of your group discussion?
Can you explain the idea you heard from someone else?
Can you say how two ideas you heard today are different or similar to each other?

Can you say how you would decide between two different points of view?

12 **Select and use appropriate registers for effective communication**

LI: To use different sorts of talk in different settings. *(Role play reporting an incident to a friend, a police officer, a parent, a much younger child, on the phone, in the playground, in the classroom, etc.)*

PD: Why do we use different sorts of talk in different settings?
What's the difference between talking to a friend and talking to a teacher?
Who can you talk to without worrying about what you say and how you say it?
Why is it important to make sure we don't (for example) use swear words in class?

THE BENEFITS OF TALK FOR LEARNING

The National Curriculum requirements are helpful in that they entitle every child to have access to the rich resources of spoken language, and not just entitle children but mandate that teachers teach children how to use specific sorts of talk effectively.

An Example: Talk for Learning at Eastwood Primary School, Bradford
In 2012, Eastwood School undertook a whole-school Talk for Learning project. Here is a section of their project evaluation:

> The focus on the development of the Talk for Learning Project throughout school has had a marked impact on pupil engagement and helped to ensure that children's language skills are central to teaching and learning across the whole curriculum. The Talk for Learning project has had a significant impact on the pupils' ability and confidence to talk and discuss their work with others and to offer guidance to their

Introduction

peers as to how to self-assess and how they might improve. Children are increasingly encouraged to see mistakes as learning points and are increasingly willing to take risks in their learning.

And an excerpt from Eastwood's 2014 Ofsted Inspection:

An emphasis on providing many opportunities for pupils to talk in lessons is helping pupils improve the quality of their writing standards in English. Pupils have plenty of opportunities to discuss their ideas and enrich their vocabulary. This is successfully fostering their English as an additional language and helping them achieve well. [...] An emphasis on learning through talk caters well for the needs of the vast majority of pupils who learn English as an additional language, as well as other pupils in school.

And finally an Eastwood child's perspective:

The teachers give us some really fun activities to solve and do. [And] when we do our talk activities they ask for our opinion.

USING THIS BOOK

The activities are offered for you to adapt in ways that will suit you and your class. There is a progression in talk skills which is built into the structure of the book. However, many of the activities can be used in any order to suit what you feel your class needs and what fits with topics you are teaching.

It is particularly important to teach about, discuss and establish class **Ground Rules for Talk**, as we describe in Chapter 1, before expecting children to work together in their groups. Otherwise your hopes of hearing exciting and interesting discussion may be dashed. Fortunately the relevant skills for discussion are readily taught and learned, and the rules, like all good rules, become obvious once you've thought of them.

Introduction

Here is a summary of what you will find in *Jumpstart! Talk for Learning*:

PART 1 Learning through talk

The first part of the book provides activities which can help your class to develop essential talk skills.

Chapter 1 Talking and learning provides a description of Exploratory Talk, as well as a series of activities which will help you to raise awareness of the importance of talk for learning, and build up a set of skills that will enable every child to take an active part in discussion. This chapter explains how to create a unique set of class Ground Rules for Talk with your class.

Chapter 2 Listening and learning has a clear focus on the skills children need so they can listen and learn from what they hear, and suggests direct teaching of active listening. By making the link between listening and learning explicit, and by offering children opportunities to say why they find listening difficult, individuals and groups can develop their capacity to listen and learn.

Chapter 3 Assessment and progression continues the focus on looking at language structures and the important skills for talk that children need to learn and practise. This chapter looks at important issues of progression and assessment.

PART 2 Curriculum activities and games

The second part suggests contexts for more specific teaching of language structures and skills.

Chapter 4 Opinions, argument and persuasion provides ideas for direct teaching of skills, and contexts for practice.

Chapter 5 Conveying information provides ideas for direct teaching of skills, and contexts for practice in descriptions, recounting, reporting, instructing, and explaining.

Chapter 6 Talk across the curriculum takes a look at National Curriculum subjects, with suggestions of what sort of talk is appropriate and useful, and what contexts can be used.

Chapter 7 Talk about stories, poems and drama has ideas for talk-focused activities and collaborative learning which can be used and re-purposed to suit the topics you are teaching. We look at oral stories and poems and offer practical suggestions; we also look at games and activities for drama and improvisation.

Chapter 8 Summary and resources provides an overview of *Talk for Learning* and suggests other resources.

PART 1
Learning through talk

CHAPTER 1
Talking and learning

> What I enjoy [...] is speaking and listening to other people; you have to look at them to see if what you are saying is having an impact.
>
> Maliha

When we are thinking about learning, some ways of talking are more useful than others. The term **exploratory talk** describes a particularly useful sort of talk in which children engage one another in a good discussion. This involves pooling all their ideas, listening actively, asking for and giving reasons, and challenging what others say in a respectful manner. Children work to gain agreement by using talk to negotiate and make meaning with one another.

Exploratory talk can be simply taught and learned, so that the child can use the necessary skills in learning. We assume that children know how to engage one another in exploratory talk at our peril. Such discussion seems simple. Indeed most children, asked to describe a good discussion, will readily point out some of the key features. And yet many children (many people) cannot hold an effective exploratory discussion, and never see the need to do so; many children may never have taken part in exploratory talk. For the child in the classroom, the risks of offering their knowledge, giving reasons and challenging others are too great, unless everyone else understands that this leads to learning, and is able and willing to do the same.

It is unusual to find a teacher involved in the direct teaching of the talk skills necessary for group discussion. As teachers, we may assume that children already have these skills – that when talking with others, they can take turns, ask one another appropriate questions, explain their own thinking and compare their point of view with others in a reasoned way. Indeed they may be able to do all of these things when an adult or mentor is with their group, but left to themselves, groups of children find it really difficult to sustain reasoned discussion. This is why they need direct tuition. They need to become aware that their discussion is crucial to their own education and that of their group. They also need to be aware that by engaging one another in exploratory talk, they are learning to reason together – and enhancing their individual capacity to reason when faced with problems.

Here are two comments from children who had experienced spoken language lessons and activities called 'Talking Time':

> I liked the talking because we discussed it properly. We decided what we should put in our books.
> David

> I don't like the talking time because Stacey just sits there.
> Adam

Adam's comment highlights Stacey's inability to join in, therefore her need for direct tuition in the relevant spoken language skills; and the problems children face when they want to discuss ideas but group members don't know how to, or have no motivation to do so. These are serious issues for the teacher, who went on to address them on Stacey's behalf – ensuring that this child had a voice in the classroom, and could go on to engage others in useful discussions. The teacher taught the children the structures of exploratory talk.

Exploratory talk is talk in which every child:

1 joins in, and asks each other to join in;
2 listens attentively and reflects on what they hear;
3 offers ideas and opinions openly, giving reasons;
4 elaborates on ideas and links ideas together;
5 works towards a negotiated outcome.

Teaching exploratory talk skills involves a series of lessons focused on these ideas, as listed opposite:

1 *Being part of a group* – what we can contribute; our expertise and what we can offer, e.g. being a good listener, being good at questioning, our general knowledge, being friendly, being capable of reasoning and so on.
2 *Listening to one another* – practising the skills of active listening.
3 *Reasoning* – asking for, and giving, reasons; comparing ideas; changing our mind when offered sound reasons to do so.
4 *Explaining and elaborating* – articulating our own ideas and providing an appropriate level of detail; using appropriate vocabulary; recalling and using factual knowledge and understanding.
5 Devising and using a set of shared **Ground Rules for Talk** which incorporate the features of exploratory talk, for group discussion with peers.

The next section provides an example of some practical steps you can work through to raise children's awareness of the importance of talk, to build up the skills needed for exploratory talk, and to create and use class Ground Rules for Talk.

RAISING AWARENESS OF THE IMPORTANCE OF TALK

Raise awareness of the importance of Talk for Learning

Talk needs a context; in this example, the context for talk is 'Lunchtime at School'. Alternatively you can use any context that is relevant to your class: a current school issue, a topic-based subject or a topic suggested by the class. The idea is to help the children become aware of talk and its power to stimulate thinking.

Ask the children to spend a minute thinking to themselves about their personal experience of lunchtime at school. Stress that you will want to know what everyone thinks. If possible, link this to a genuine context such as informing the school council of suggestions, or putting information for parents on the school website.

Display these questions on the following page:

What do you like about lunchtimes at school?

What would you change?

Do you know anything about what other children do in other schools?

Next ask children to predict what they think others will say. They can make a note if necessary. Ask them:

How easy or difficult is it to do this?

Can they tell what others are thinking?

Model how to share ideas by asking a confident pair or group to share their ideas aloud. Point out good practice such as listening, taking turns and asking questions.

Now ask children in pairs or groups to share their ideas, taking turns to speak and listen. After a few minutes stop the class and ask children individually to say what they have heard – that is, what others think. Ask for any ideas that were a surprise, or not what they would have predicted.

Ask a child to explain their own ideas clearly to the class, then ask them to say if this is made easier by their discussion time. Highlight the importance of talk for communicating ideas, and the importance of others as careful listeners.

Finally, ask children to say if they found the ideas interesting or useful, and decide what can be done with all the new information that has been aired.

Point out the value of talk for learning. Ask children for examples from their own experience of times when they have learned through talk. (They may find this difficult at this stage.) Introduce the idea of a link between talking and thinking; and between thinking and learning. Explain that the class are going to learn to use talk to think aloud together.

Other suggested contexts for raising awareness of Talk for Learning

Bullying; safe use of the Internet; making friends; birthday parties; what we're looking forward to; early memories of starting school; my hobby; transferring to a new class/school; learning out of school; my favourite relative; the best thing about weekends.

Continue to raise awareness of Talk for Learning

Keeping a focus on talking, thinking and learning, use the resource *A classroom conversation about Talk for Learning* to stimulate discussion and raise awareness. This can be a whole-class session, or the children can be given the questions to discuss with a group or at home first, before contributing to a class discussion. After the talk, ask children to sum up what they have heard, or to say what has been thought-provoking or interesting.

A classroom conversation about Talk for Learning

Who thinks they are a talkative person?
Who thinks they are a quiet person?
Who do you like talking to? Why?
When are you asked not to talk? Why?
What does 'chatterbox' mean?
Do you like talking on the phone? Who do you talk to?
What's the difference between talk, email and texts?
When is it really helpful to be able to talk to people? Why?
When is it difficult to talk to other people?
What do you like to talk about with your friends?
What sort of things can we do in school by talking together?
Are you asked to talk together in class? In which lessons? Why?
Can you think of reasons why talking is useful?
What 'jobs' can people get done by talking to each other?
How would you communicate with other people if you couldn't talk?
How many different languages can you speak?
How many different languages have you heard of?
What happens when people talk but others don't listen?
What are any differences between talking and writing?
Can people be taught how to talk to one another?
What learning happens through talk?
What sort of talk can help learning when we are doing group work?

TEACHING EXPLORATORY TALK SKILLS

In essence, children need to be taught skills to:

- include everyone in the group;
- share all knowledge and ideas openly;
- ask for and give reasons;
- challenge what others say in a respectful manner;
- sum up and come to an agreement.

Some of your children may have some or all of these skills. But unless all children are aware of their importance, children may never apply their skills in a discussion with classmates unless a teacher is present. The idea is to develop their independence by teaching every child an awareness of how important their individual contribution is, and the skills to contribute.

The key talk skills above will become the Learning Intentions (LIs) for your talk lessons. Since a context for talk is needed, here we use a **science** topic as an example. Each of these five sample activities addresses science curriculum aims, and simultaneously teaches children crucial talk skills. Each of the five sessions should last about 15 to 20 minutes including the plenary, unless you feel that more time would be of value.

It's possible to teach these talk lessons in any curriculum context; see Chapter 6 for further suggestions.

Keep writing/recording to an absolute minimum; the focus is on talk.

TALK FOR LEARNING IN SCIENCE: HABITATS

(with children in exploratory groups)

> A habitat is a place which has the right conditions for a plant or animal to live.
>
> It may be very small, such as under a leaf or stone, or large, such as a tree or pond.

1 Everyone has a voice
Learning Intentions:

- To include everyone in the group
- To identify habitats around the school

Share the Learning Intentions. Ask children to suggest ways that they can make sure everyone in the group has a chance to speak. Establish some clear strategies, such as taking turns, or passing round a card or object for the speaker to hold. Ask children to say how they know if someone is listening to them. Tell the children that your plenary will involve asking them to share something that they heard in their discussion.

Ask children in their groups to take it in turns to suggest (without writing down) a place around the school/gardens/park/village/town/local area where something wild might live. It can be a plant or an animal. Between them they should suggest six habitats and at least one living thing for each habitat.

Plenary: Ask children to tell you what others in their group suggested. Ask them to provide examples of good listening and turn-taking.

2 All knowledge is shared
Learning Intentions:

- To share all ideas openly
- To think together about living things in their habitats

Share the LIs. Ask groups to identify the **barriers** to sharing ideas. Bring out misconceptions about 'cheating' and 'showing off'. Establish the idea that everyone does better if we all pool what we know rather than keeping it to ourselves. Ask if they can think of some examples of when that is evident. Ask groups to use their turn-taking and listening skills – and to include everyone – to share everything they know about the conditions in two habitats of their choice. What are the particular conditions in terms of shelter, light, water, temperature, seasonal changes, food availability?

Plenary: Ask specific children to provide information about their habitat on behalf of their group. Ask children: who in their group is good at sharing, or has helpful ideas, listens carefully or ensures everyone is included?

3 Reasoning
Learning Intentions:

- To ask for and give reasons
- To say **why** animals or plants live in their habitats

Share the LIs. Model the use of the word 'because' for giving reasons. Ask children to pass around a card which says *What do you think? Why do you think that?* in their group, taking turns to speak and listen. This can help the focus on reasoning. Ask children to discuss a particular habitat – one that they have established, or a habitat that you suggest for the whole class – and its living things. Think about the conditions in the habitat; discuss how these suit particular living things, providing what is needed to survive and raise young or set seed.

> **Tree habitat**
>
> The tree provides a range of habitats at different heights, on different sides of the tree, in tree holes, in roots and bark, under leaves. An oak tree supports hundreds of creatures. In or on the tree live mosses, lichens, ladybirds, woodlice, centipedes, squirrels, a variety of birds and moths; others rely on the tree for shelter, such as deer and badger; or eat its leaves, like caterpillars and worms.

Plenary: Ask children to give examples from their group of a living thing, its habitat and why the habitat is suitable. Ask children to suggest examples of good reasons, or reasons which helped them to think more deeply or change their mind. Point out that 'changing your mind' is a real advantage when it means you have learned something.

Ask individuals to share what they have heard, and ask groups to say how well their group took turns or shared information. Ask if anyone can say something they have learned from a classmate.

4 Challenge and argument
Learning Intentions:

- To challenge what others say in a respectful manner
- To consider some ideas about habitat loss

Share the LIs. Explain the difference between argument as a useful means to make sense of things, and an angry and destructive 'argument'. Model how to challenge others with respect. If needed, provide cards with these talk tools:

> 'I agree with – because'
>
> 'I disagree with – because'

Learning through talk

Read, display or present the 'Beech Grove' scenario to set up a context for discussion in this session.

Ask the groups to discuss their ideas. They can choose one person to be a house builder, one to be a campaigner for saving the woodland and one to be a badger. Talking in role will affect what they can say: they may prefer simply to state their own ideas; but in this activity there must be some difference of opinion.

Beech Grove Housing Plan

People need homes. The government has said that the Town Council has to build 250 homes in the local area. The Council has looked at where the houses can go. The choice is between the school playing field, a field which has a large pond, an old factory site and Beech Grove woodland.

The Council has decided that Beech Grove is the best place to build.

It is cheaper to cut down the trees than it is to clear the old factory site, which is full of dangerous chemicals. The pond has been found to have rare Great Crested Newts, very expensive to move, and the school does not want to lose its playing field.

Is this the best decision?

Talking points: Beech Grove Housing Plan

People need houses and we can't let trees get in the way of building.

There are plenty of places badgers can go if we dig up the woodland.

Trees should never be cut down to suit people.

Discuss these statements, thinking of as many ideas to offer as possible.

Plenary: Ask groups to say whether they found it possible to agree and disagree with one another, and what problems they encountered. What difference did giving a reason make? Ask groups to give examples of how their group discussed the ideas, or ask one group to role play their discussion.

Ask groups to record one sentence or picture in response to each of the statements. (They can write, audio record or draw.) This summary will be used in the next activity.

5 Summing up, a group decision
Learning Intentions:

- To sum up and come to an agreement
- To think creatively about habitats

Share the LIs. In this session, the summaries from session 4 are used by the whole class. Ask each group to share their sentences or pictures. These could be displayed around the room for all to look at. Then ask groups to discuss the following scenario, and think together to create a summary of points of view and a group response to the problem of competition for the woodland habitat.

Summary: Beech Grove Housing Plan

Talk together to decide on what your group thinks are TWO especially important points of view about building on a woodland habitat.

Use your own ideas and the whole-class ideas to make up two sentences or drawings that show **completely opposite** points of view.

Make up a song, poem, story, rap, presentation, list, drawing or design to clarify these two ideas for the class.

Finally think together to create what your group thinks is a really good solution to the problem. This can be very practical, or imaginative or even magical − but it must be clearly described. Add this solution to your presentation.

Plenary: Ask groups to say how they went about summing up ideas. Ask individuals to give an evaluation of how effectively their group worked. Keep this positive – ask for strong points, or difficulties that were resolved.

Ask groups to present their rehearsed ideas to the class.

CREATING CLASS GROUND RULES FOR TALK

Learning Intentions:

- To create a set of rules for effective talk

Activity
Ask groups to discuss their ideas and make up three rules which will help them to talk effectively and learn together; record these rules on sticky notes.

Collect all the notes in.

Ask groups to label their group members A, B and C.

Ask Cs to change groups. Once everyone is settled, ask As to change groups too, making sure they don't go to the same group as their original C person. Now give three random sticky notes to each new group.

Ask the new groups to read the rules. Do they agree or disagree with them? Ask the new groups to rewrite any rules they think need to change, and to add one more rule that they think important.

Plenary: Ask a group to read out one rule. Stick this rule on a surface. Ask the next group for a different rule. Read it and stick it on a different surface. As the sticky notes are read and groups read out similar rules, these should be placed in a set with the ones they match. You will end up with sets of rules.

Take all the notes from one set onto a sheet of paper.

Clarify, summarise each set into one rule in the children's own language, and record.

You should devise about six rules which reflect the summary of exploratory talk given at the start of this chapter.

Share the rules in a whole-class session. Ask the class to say whether they feel they now have all the rules they need for a good discussion, or if there is anything to add.

These rules are your all-important and unique class **Ground Rules for Exploratory Talk**.

Use them all the time.

Provide each child with a paper copy of their rules. Display the final list around the room, and send it home for discussion with parents and carers. Generally refer to and use the class rules to promote good discussion. The rules should be revised if the class sees the need to do so. Also the class should be regularly asked to evaluate use of rules in discussion, and their own developing talk skills.

An example of class Ground Rules for Talk (Year 5)

We include everyone in the group when we talk together.

Everyone must give ideas.

We ask each other for reasons.

We can disagree with ideas if we have a good reason.

We try to solve problems or decide things together.

CHAPTER 2
Listening and learning

> I like talking time because it has helped me to listen a bit more and I have got better at talking.
>
> *Ben*

Listening seems so straightforward and obvious a skill that we do not often take time to stop and provide some direct teaching about it. But children need to learn how to listen attentively, reflecting on what they hear, and organising their thoughts so that they can contribute to a discussion. They need to learn to focus on the task in hand. They also need to understand that listening is important to their classmates; and that as they listen to others, they will be listened to. Listening attentively is a powerful gift to offer a speaker, and can help children's social relationships as much as their learning. Children need chances to say what they think about listening, and to suggest ways that activities in school can be organised so that they can listen with less difficulty. They need to be able to evaluate their own skills as a listener, and to be able to use what they have heard.

RAISING AWARENESS OF PARTICULAR LISTENING SKILLS

You can provide questions about the skills of listening, either in a whole-class setting or for small groups to discuss, with or without adult support. You can use a questionnaire, interview format, homework or class discussion to find out what the children think about 'listening', in a way that will help you to teach them what they need to know about how and why to listen.

> **Questions about listening**
>
> Can you tell if people are listening to you? How?
>
> What do you like to listen to?
>
> When is it difficult to listen, and why?
>
> Who would you describe as a good listener, and why?
>
> What helps you to listen better?
>
> What sounds do you not like to listen to?
>
> What is the difference between sound, noise, music and talk?
>
> Can people learn to listen?
>
> Can you say what 'active listening' means?
>
> What is the link between listening and thinking?
>
> What is the link between listening and learning?

Instead of questions, you can phrase ideas as statements for discussion – *Talking points*. Discuss these points in small groups before feedback to the whole class.

Talking points: Listening

Do you and your group agree or disagree with these ideas? Say why.

Listening to other people talking can be very boring.

Listening is important.

Listening is something you do without thinking.

You are good at listening, or not, and nothing can be done about it.

Listening helps you speak.

You can learn by listening.

It is difficult to listen in the classroom.

> *People can help you to listen.*
>
> *Listening carefully can make things more interesting.*
>
> *We can make up a good definition of the phrase, 'Active Listening'.*
>
> *Listening is for grown-ups.*

LISTENING ACTIVITIES

This section provides some examples of listening activities. The focus is on what is heard, and what the child subsequently does with it. For each activity, finish with a plenary, asking children to reflect on:

- how easy or difficult it is to listen;
- whether they enjoy listening;
- what makes listening impossible;
- what they think they have learned by listening.

Listening Learning Intention

In parallel with your curriculum Learning Intentions, use a listening Learning Intention such as 'We are going to use active listening'; 'We are going to listen and think'; 'We are going to listen and then make a suggestion'; 'We are going to listen and remember'. Use a Learning Intention for the whole class, or target specific children.

In your Plenary Discussion, ask children to give examples of effective listening and learning they have experienced. You will be aware of the problems your class has with listening and can generate appropriate Learning Intentions. These might be quite general, like the one you chose above. Or they can deal with finer detail, for example: 'I will look at the person speaking'; 'We are going to repeat what we have heard'; 'We will look, listen and then respond'; 'We will show that we have listened by commenting on what was said/using it to do an activity/sharing ideas with our group'.

Listening in PE
Use sound signals in PE. For example:

one whistle = Stop!

clap hands = Listen!

double whistle = Go!

Ask children to note who is good at listening, how they can tell, and what difference it makes to the game.

Mobile
Ask children to make up a mobile phone conversation to share with the class. This can be between historical characters, story book characters, animals, aliens or a role play about visitors, bullying and so on. Talk about listening, questioning, misunderstanding and the impact of listening while doing a separate activity.

Sound out
Ask children to listen to sound-effects and identify what they hear using a range of vocabulary.

Listening vocabulary

Discuss, display, illustrate and use this vocabulary.

Volume: noisy, loud, quiet

Pitch: high, low

Rhythm: regular, irregular

Instruments: percussion, stringed, wind

Music: tune, rhythm, beat, tempo, waltz, march

Noise: loud, crash, boom, explosion

Quiet: whisper, hush, silence

Listen to a story
Read a short story, or story introduction, displaying key words and characters in print. Ask children to retell the story to a partner, taking turns and helping one another to recall detail and the order of events.

Ask one child to start telling the story and then 'pass it on' to another until the story has been retold by everyone in the class.

Ask children to draw a picture based on a story that is read out loud. Perhaps the children can ask questions to check on details.

Listen to a song
Listen to a song which has a narrative or clear repetitive phrases. Ask children to tell each other what they heard. Ask children to make up questions about the song to ask other groups in a whole-class setting. Ask children to make up a song or chant for themselves.

Listen to music
Listen to a short piece of music. Ask children to tap out the rhythm. Ask if they can identify any instruments playing.

Play another piece of music. Ask children to discuss with their partner which music they enjoy more, and why.

Later in the day, ask children if they can hum or sing the air or tune.

Ask children to recall if they have heard the music before, and when.

Use and discuss words like pitch, tone, volume, rhythm, tune.

Listen to a rhyming poem
Read a poem which has clear rhymes. Ask children, with a partner, to say what rhyming words they heard. Ask them to choose two words that rhyme and make up a rhyming couplet of their own to say to the class.

Read out the poem again, stopping before the ends of lines; ask children to contribute the rhymes as they occur.

Listen and write
Read, slowly and clearly, a paragraph containing class spellings, science vocabulary, new or interesting words. Ask children to write words or check them off on a list.

Listen and draw
Read a factual description or list. Ask children to draw what they hear. Share drawings and ask children to evaluate details and say what they found difficult about listening.

What makes which sound?
Display pictures of sound sources (animal, computer, TV, musical instruments, people talking, machines). Ask children to create describing words and add to the display.

Use the words in a story or poem.

Listening ears
Collect and look at pictures of mammal ears, e.g. cat, rabbit, fennec fox, bat, elephant, mouse. Find out how our hearing works. Find out what helps hearing, and what things can damage hearing. Ask children to wear ear muffs to simulate loss of hearing and discuss the importance of our hearing as a sense. Link hearing, listening, thinking and responding. Look at and discuss hearing impairment in children and adults.

Change the form
Immediately after listening to a story, ask the children to present it in a different form. A story written in the third person can be presented from the point of view of one of the characters, or the story can be turned into a play. Similarly, a set of instructions can be turned into a rap. A recount of an event can be turned into a ballad.

What do you know?

This is a listening activity to help introduce a new topic. Ask the children to work in groups and give each group a large sheet of paper. Tell the children the topic. Ask them to draw three columns and label them 'What we already know'; 'What we would like to know'; and 'What we have learned'. In groups, the children discuss what they already know and what they would like to know, filling in the first two columns. Then you provide initial input into the new topic, for example by giving an oral presentation, showing a video, etc. After listening to you or watching the video, the children talk to one another to recall information, to describe what they have seen and heard, or to say what they thought; they then fill in the third column together.

This could be an individual activity, and indeed it may be useful to ask individuals to complete the columns first, then compare notes as they work in a group.

Listeners of the Week

This activity introduces an element of competition for groups, as they try to become 'Listeners of the Week'. During a week, ask groups to focus on several listening challenges. For example, read the class a story and check which group can remember events most accurately. Similarly, read an article from a newspaper, listen to an item from a radio broadcast, read a narrative poem or an extract from a non-fiction book. Children should not make notes while they are listening, but afterwards they should talk together to note down what they can recall. Award groups marks out of ten, or smiley faces, for each listening activity. The winning group can be asked to talk to the class about 'what makes a good listener'; or to choose their own groups for the following week's challenges.

Summing up

Invite an adult to give a short talk to the class. It could be a parent talking about a job or hobby, a grandparent talking about their school days, or a professional talking about some aspect of school life of interest to the children. Tell the children that after they have listened to the talk, you will be asking them to sum up what they have learned from it. Again, children should not make notes while they are listening, but afterwards talk together to note down what they can recall. Invite the groups to (a) devise questions which can be put to the speaker orally or in writing, and (b) prepare an oral report lasting no more than two minutes in which they give a summary of what the speaker said.

FEEDBACK AND THE IMPORTANCE OF LISTENING

Ask a child to prepare a short talk or presentation. The subject can be their hobby, a story, a country, an animal, a place. After listening to the talk, ask the other children in the class to feed back what they learned from the talk.

Discuss listening, using vocabulary such as *attentive, active, thoughtful*. Ask what the children find difficult about listening, and what they perceive as barriers to listening. Discuss what makes a good environment for listening and what does not. Make explicit the links between speaking, listening, thinking and learning.

Ensure that every child is given the chance to present. Some children may need to do this as a pair until they become confident enough to present alone. This confidence is built as children experience a friendly, interested audience in their classmates.

CHAPTER 3
Assessment and progression

The psychologist Jerome Bruner tells us that a child of any age is capable of understanding complex information:

> We begin with the hypothesis that any subject can be taught effectively in some intellectually honest form to any child at any stage of development.
> (Bruner, 1960, *The Process of Education*)

The choice of what talk skills to teach, and therefore what to assess, depends on your understanding of the child's need. This chapter provides some ideas for assessment for you to adapt to your own purposes.

What can we usefully assess?
Talk is not a homogeneous thing; any register of talk will have its own distinctive features. In order to assess talk, you will need to identify specific features or structures, and decide which are to be the focus for your teaching and assessment. This chapter identifies such features in some different types of talk. We can usefully assess the aspects of talk that we think are of value, such as:

- reasoning, explaining and elaborating;
- clarity and coherence of presentation;
- ability to argue a point.

We can also assess active listening.

Why assess spoken language?
It is useful to assess spoken language so that you can target future teaching, and so that you can help children to note their own

progression in competence. You will know which talk skills your children need help with, and at what level. Assessment provides both teacher and child with a marker of the current state of affairs; knowing where you are allows planning for development. Assessment enables you to pass on considered information that may be useful to a parent or another teacher.

Who can assess spoken language?
When we speak to people in an everyday way, what we say is often informally assessed for its meaning, its content, its clarity, its purpose and so on. We all assess one another through what is said, on a daily basis. We also note how well others listen to us.

In school, however, assessment is a more specific activity, looking at particular aspects of spoken language, especially when there has been direct input for a child or group or if there is some concern over a child's development. Assessment in class helps children to discern their progress, and helps teachers to target future input for individuals and groups. Teachers, teaching assistants, other professionals in the classroom, parents and carers, can all assess spoken language. Crucially, the child can also assess both their own talk and that of their classmates. Self-assessment and peer assessment can be taught as skills.

It is particularly important that children are taught how to look for the best in their peers, how to describe what is well done, and how to make positive and encouraging suggestions about future work. Children should never be allowed to disparage one another's spoken language but should have the skills and understanding to point out good use of language for discussion, explanation, presentation and so on.

What not to assess?
This book is not concerned with either changing or assessing a child's accent or dialect, both of which are irrelevant when it comes to developing thinking. A child's own language is an essential link with a community of speakers and listeners. We do suggest that children can usefully build up a repertoire of ways of talking which are useful in different circumstances, and that the

way of talking we call *exploratory talk* is particularly useful in educational settings.

We have not focused on Standard English, and we have not included specific material about the learning of English as an Additional Language, or the teaching of languages such as French, German or Spanish. It is apparent that children with more than one language have a greater range of resources for thinking to draw on, and that they have the capacity to make meaning in more comprehensive ways. However, that is not the focus of this book and we leave assessment of such enviable capacity to others.

How often to assess; and who for?

Assessment of talk skills – such as giving opinions, taking part in arguments or using persuasion – can be a single 'snapshot' or a gradual process of accumulating information. There is so much to assess that you may have to make difficult decisions if your assessments are going to be accurate enough to be of value for planning future teaching. So, for example, you may assess descriptive talk systematically, keeping records for each child; and you may assess debating skills informally, taking note of what seems apparent on one occasion only.

Any assessment of talk is worthwhile, as long as you are clear about your focus for teaching, the linked focus for assessment and the impact this will have on planning or reporting. You, your team of colleagues and your school will have specific priorities for the teaching and learning of spoken language; and your children will have particular skills and particular needs. Once you've clarified what it is the children need and what you are going to teach them, you can make decisions about what and how to assess – and what to do with the information you gather.

ASSESSMENT QUESTIONS FOR A RANGE OF TYPES OF TALK

This section lists questions which can be used as tick-lists or in interview schedules. Each question deals with a particular skill which can be a teaching focus in lessons, if you feel that this is the area in which the child needs help.

> **Presentational talk – teacher's assessment**
> Did the talk have a good beginning?
>
> Was the information interesting enough to hold the audience's attention?
>
> Was the talk easy to understand?
>
> Was the content organised in a logical sequence?
>
> Did the speaker make good use of technology, e.g. PowerPoint slides?
>
> Was the talk an appropriate length of time?
>
> Did the talk have a good ending?
>
> Did you learn something from the talk?
>
> Did the presenter give clear answers to questions?
>
> Was there anything about the talk that particularly impressed you?
>
> What does the presenter need to work on so that they can improve the content and structure of their talks?

Presentational talk – self-assessment

Did you hold the audience's attention?

Was your voice audible, and was the pace even and steady?

Did the audience understand the information?

Did the talk have a good beginning?

Did you use appropriate body language and gestures?

Did the different parts of the talk link together well?

Did you aim to appear confident, and maintain confidence?

Did you hesitate at all and, if so, why do you think this happened?

Did you make good use of technology in your presentation?

Was the talk the right length of time?

Did it have a good ending?

Were you able to answer any questions asked?

Which parts of the presentation went well?

What could you work on to improve future presentations?

Presentational talk – peer assessment
Was the talk presented clearly?

Did the speaker talk clearly and at an appropriate volume?

Was the speaker generally fluent, and able to continue after hesitating?

Did the speaker make eye-contact with the audience?

Did the speaker read the information, or did they talk without reading very much?

Did the speaker use any visual aids? If so, were they clear?

Was the talk delivered confidently?

Did the speaker use body language effectively during the talk?

What impressed you about the delivery of the talk?

What could the speaker do to improve their next talk?

Presenting an argument – self-assessment

Is your argument developed point by point in an organised way?

Do you grab the audience's attention and involve them in what you say?

Do you quote facts and statistics to support your view?

Do you listen and respond to others?

Do you pick up points made by others in favour of your viewpoint?

Do you draw on your own experience to support your view?

Do you quote what others have said in support of your view?

Do you express how strongly you feel about the issue?

Do you pick out the main points and conclude with a summary of them?

Do you use your body language – e.g., gestures and facial expressions – to try to influence people to accept your argument?

What could you do in the future to improve your ability to present an argument?

Listening skills – teacher's assessment
Does the child look at you and appear to listen?

Does the child reflect on what they hear?

Can the child respond appropriately to a direct question?

Does the child make relevant comments or suggestions?

Is the child easily distracted by others, by noise or by their surroundings?

Can they recall key facts or ideas later?

Does the child focus on the subject, or do they make lateral remarks?

Can the child follow verbal instructions?

Does the child listen well to adults and to other children?

Does the child hear when talk is at an appropriate volume?

Can they listen to music, radio or a presentation – for increasing lengths of time?

Listening skills – self-assessment
Give yourself a mark from 1 to 5, where 1 = sometimes, 5 = always

Do you give the person who is speaking your full attention?

Do you think about what you hear?

Do you interrupt if you disagree with what is being said?

Are you easily distracted by other people, noise or the surroundings?

Do you wait for people to finish or for the chairperson to invite you to speak?

Do you keep focused on the topic being discussed?

Can you challenge an argument by quoting someone's reasons and saying why you disagree with them?

Can you identify the main points that are made and summarise them?

Are you prepared to listen to others' arguments and change your mind if they argue convincingly?

Can you think of and ask appropriate questions?

Can you recall what you heard, later?

What do you think makes a good listener?

How could you improve your listening skills?

Assessment and progression

Listening skills – peer assessment
Give your classmate a mark out of 5 for listening, where 1= sometimes, 5= always

Looks at who is talking

Attends by keeping still and quiet

Makes an effort to listen and learn

Answers questions sensibly

Can say what the talk was about

Can think of questions to ask

Takes no notice of distractions like noise or other people

Remembers some important facts or words

Can tell how the speaker is feeling

Is open-minded and prepared to accept new ideas or change their mind

ASSESSING GROUP DISCUSSION SKILLS

A child needs to learn to listen attentively, take turns, invite others to contribute, speak clearly and say things that are to the point. In addition, they need to be able to share ideas, explain, elaborate, draw on what they hear as the discussion continues and to negotiate an agreement. They need to be able to see that others may have a valid point of view, and that good evidence or a good argument can be enough to help them change their mind. They need the skills to sum up the discussion and report back to a wider group. This is a complex combination of skills, but the separate capacities can be taught – and assessed – separately to help the child build up to full participation in group discussion.

Assessment of discussion skills can be straightforward – it can simply involve having a 'talk' Learning Intention *in parallel with* your curriculum Learning Intention. You will ask the class to suggest, in your Plenary Discussion session, who they think explained something well, or listened carefully or gave a good reason – whatever was your original focus. This foregrounding of success is a good experience for both the child nominated, and the child who has made the evaluation.

Example: **Talk LI + Curriculum LI (Science)**
Talk LI: to ask a question and listen to the answer
Science LI: to understand that magnets attract some metals

Alternatively, you can use group discussion time to listen to an individual child or to a pair or group, noting what they achieve and what they find difficult. You can ask children to take turns to be 'Listener', joining a talk group to make a note of who did what well. It's a good idea to give the Listener a focus such as noting who used the word 'because', who spoke clearly, who stayed on task. Or they could complete a simple tally of who spoke. Their findings should always be reported positively.

AUDITING A CHILD'S DISCUSSION SKILLS

You can use a chart to keep a record of a child's developing discussion skills. The example here is designed to be used once every half-term, but can be adapted to the pattern of your school year, or to the talk focus of your lessons.

You can simply tick the box, or you can use a scale of numbers such as *1 never, 2 occasionally, 3 sometimes, 4 frequently, 5 always* so that if a child listens attentively much of the time in their first half-term, you would put '4' in the first box of the first row.

Discussion skills audit

Child's name:

Skill	HALF-TERM					
	1	2	3	4	5	6
Listens attentively						
Takes turns						
Invites others to contribute						
Speaks clearly						
Respects the ideas of others						
Shares ideas and information						
Gives reasons for what they say						
Explains clearly						
Elaborates on own ideas and others' ideas						

(continued)

Chains ideas together					
Negotiates different points of view					
Sums up the discussion					
Reports back orally to a wider group					

ASSESSING SPECIALISED TALK

Chapter 4 of this book looks at specialised ways of talking: opinions, argument, persuasion, debate.

Chapter 5 looks at: describing, recounting, reporting, instructing and explaining.

Each of these specialised sorts of spoken language has particular structures which you can teach separately, in your curriculum lessons, and assess.

For example, we can list some key features of descriptive talk (Chapter 5) as:

1 Using accurate vocabulary

2 Providing effective simile, metaphor and imagery – figurative language – to help the listener to visualise, hear, touch or taste things

3 Bringing something to life by portraying it clearly and enthusiastically

4 Presenting information in an orderly and logical sequence

5 Checking for understanding in the listener

6 Being concise without leaving out key details.

You can teach and assess each of these features separately, building up the child's capacity to describe things, and their self-evaluation of their skill. Children can use the key features of talk to think about areas of their own competence, and to evaluate and provide supportive feedback for their classmates. You can make a chart based on the 'Discussion Skills Audit' (page 35) chart to keep a track of progress over time. You can focus on one type of talk for half a term, making sure that every child gains confidence and skills, before moving on to focus on the next type of talk.

PROGRESSION IN TALK SKILLS

Looking at talk is like looking at a fractal picture – focusing on one aspect of it makes it apparent that the picture can be seen in even finer detail, ad infinitum. It's important that an idea of progression is built into planning and teaching, with the proviso that talk skills are rarely learned sequentially, and there may be no particular order in which to learn a competence in, for example, reasoning. Yet discerning progression in talk skills involves deciding on a 'starting' level of detail. Here are two examples of such progression: in (1) reasoning and (2) listening.

You could usefully write your own versions of what you consider to be progression in these skills, or any talk skill you wish to teach and assess, such as explaining, elaborating, persuading, negotiating.

Listening – a progression

passive/not listening – ignoring, looking away, not attending

pretend listening – using body language or words to imply listening while primarily occupied in thinking about something else

selective listening – *intentionally* disregarding or dismissing the other person's views; gratuitous disagreement or agreement

misunderstanding listening – *unconsciously* overlaying own ideas; hearing only part of what has been said

empathic listening – listening and responding to check facts and feelings

attentive listening – listening and thinking, interested, taking in information

active listening – listening, reflecting, clearly understanding feelings; comprehending factual information and ideas; responding with questions and relevant comment

Reasoning – a progression

Understand that a reason means a *cause* or *connection*

Use 'because', 'if', 'perhaps' appropriately

Understand that because we all have different histories and experiences, we have different points of view and so can give different reasons

Use 'I think', 'I believe', 'I understand', 'I know' to give reasons

Understand that we can ask for and give reasons

Use 'Why?' questions appropriately

Use exploratory talk to discuss ideas rationally

Able to think of contrasting reasons – for and against

Use evidence or information to construct reasons

Able to evaluate reasons as more – or less – accurate, evidence-based, sensible, 'good', powerful, persuasive

Able to consider a range of reasons and discern their value for decision-making

Understand that *changing your mind*, because of reasons offered, is a way of learning

Understand that some decisions are not entirely based on reasons

SUMMARY

Assessment is useful in the teaching of talk for learning, offering the chance to identify gaps in competence and opportunities for further teaching. In addition, assessment enables us to provide more accurate reports to parents and other teachers, and to ensure that planning is relevant and is based on what the child can do. Assessment can be carried out by the teacher, by the child, or by peers – or all three – to build up a more comprehensive understanding of an individual's competence in talk. Children should be taught how to evaluate one another in positive, supportive terms, and to make suggestions for further development. This skill will help them to understand how they are judged themselves.

What to teach, and assessment of the impact of teaching, are inextricably linked. That is, decisions about lesson content have clear implications for later assessment. Returning to the words of Jerome Bruner which begin this chapter, what to teach and therefore what to assess depend on what you understand the child to need to support their development, and that in turn is based on what they can already do unaided and can do with help.

Progression in talk skills can be built in to your teaching of talk throughout a school year, term or even a week. Careful assessment can help you to discern progression and to make decisions about next steps for individual children, partners, groups or the whole class. It is useful to have some record in your planning which will help you report on progression to other teachers or to parents and carers. In addition, children who are made aware of their own progress can take pride in new skills and can begin to see how such capacities are transferable to other contexts than the classroom. For example, a child who knows that they are good at giving reasons, or clear explanations or describing things (and so on) may have the confidence to speak up for themselves in a range of situations. Becoming articulate is a long process, and the small steps taken every day in class can become important stepping stones in creating confident speakers – which is what we want all our children to be.

PART 2
Curriculum activities and games

CHAPTER 4
Opinions, argument and persuasion

> Debating is useful to me because it helps me to argue; also it helps me to listen carefully and helps me to express my ideas and fight back using strong, powerful vocabulary. It also makes me more confident.
>
> Fareeha

OPINIONS AND POINTS OF VIEW

Children require practice in expressing a range of points of view – and, crucially, listening to the points of view of others and considering what they say. Sometimes children's ideas are tentative and fluid, and easily influenced. Sometimes they have very fixed ideas about what they think, so that the ideas of others may seem to be wrong, threatening or aggressive in some way. Children need to learn the skills of offering ideas, listening to others and weighing up what they hear in order to make meaning of it. Developing this skill may take all their primary years in school, therefore teaching talk may seem daunting, but it is essential for the child that they learn how to negotiate and to articulate and evaluate their ideas in comparison with others. Direct teaching of useful skills, and appropriate language for offering opinions, can really help. Opinions are often mixed up with feelings. For the child, the chance to express their own ideas and be attended to by others is a valuable experience.

You can model a discussion in which clear opinions are given. Role play is useful here. Ask the children to listen to you and the teaching assistant talking about an issue that may interest them, for example, 'Children should not have mobile phones'. You can act simple

Curriculum activities and games

scenarios such as: (a) you both agree, with no discussion, in a rather uncaring way; (b) you have a strong disagreement and do not appear to listen to one another; (c) you both put different points of view in a reasoned way and show that it is possible to 'agree to disagree' – and that it's useful to hear what others think. Ask children to comment on the role plays and their effectiveness for sharing opinions and ideas.

Ask the children to make up and show their own role plays, on the same topic or a topic of current interest that you know will engage them.

Sharing opinions
Identify, talk about and display the appropriate language tools that will be helpful in sharing opinions. For example:

| I think   I believe   I understand   my idea is   I have heard that
| my opinion is   what do you think   can you explain about
| why do you think that   but   our ideas are the same
| our ideas are different   I can see what you mean   I don't understand
| I disagree because   I agree because   I understand |

Move from talking about ideas which are general – the mobile phone scenario – to ideas which are more personal and firmly held by the child. Ensure that different points of view are valued. Children expressing what may be considered socially unacceptable points of view such as racist or homophobic views should be listened to in the same respectful way; they may need some individual discussion time with you in order to be able to see a more libertarian point of view.

It's important to allow time for new ideas to 'incubate'. Discussions about points of view are not really end points but part of an ongoing trying out of ideas in relation to the ideas of others, and a new perspective may take some time to evolve.

Ideas for discussing opinions
Here are some ideas for discussion of opinions. Ground Rules for Talk should be used to ensure equitable and effective group work. Plenary sessions should focus on both the content of the discussion, and the children's evaluation of how well they shared ideas and opinions. It is highly possible that there will be disagreement; groups should know that this is going to happen, and that their talk together should be based on listening to and considering a range of ideas, not having to agree with everything they hear. Groups should be able to explain the nature of their disagreement in the plenary session.

These activities are suggestions – there will be many more opportunities for airing opinions, practising persuasion or using argument, in your curriculum work. The chapter closes with two short sections on the more formal topics of giving a speech, and organising a formal debate.

The best TV programme
Invite children in groups to suggest the best television programme they have seen recently. Encourage them to think of different types of programmes – chat shows, quiz shows, documentaries, talent shows, sitcoms, episodes of soaps. Ask them to take it in turns to explain to their group which programme they have chosen and why. Ask groups to discuss the programmes, thinking about what they can agree on – what opinions they share – and what ideas they do not agree about.

Ask groups to contribute to a whole-class discussion using their ideas.

Points of view
Ask the children what annoys them most about television programmes generally. For example, do they think characters in TV shows are too violent? Are there any programmes that they object to because of the way certain groups are portrayed? Is there too much swearing on TV? Are children's programmes patronising or silly? Set up the context for presentation as in a radio call-in or a TV 'Points of view' programme. Encourage groups to focus on a particular programme and to give the reasons for their opinions.

Curriculum activities and games

Pick of the week
For this activity you need copies of the TV schedules for the coming week. Give the children each a copy of the schedules and ask them individually to prepare a short statement saying which ten programmes they recommend and why. Then ask children to work in groups to discuss their ideas and sort out a 'Best schedule' for one evening. They will need to decide on their audience.

Soap operas
Ask the children in a class discussion to explain what are their favourite TV soaps and why. Ask groups to discuss *Talking points: Soap operas*, making sure that all opinions are heard. Do they agree or disagree with the statements, and why?

Encourage groups to discuss what makes a good soap and to draw up a list of the features of a good soap, then to share their ideas in a class discussion.

Talking points: Soap operas

Soap operas present a realistic picture of life.

A good soap has characters in it that you can relate to.

The storylines in soaps are far-fetched.

Real life is much more interesting than the lives shown in soaps.

People identify with the characters in soaps.

What I like about soaps is the suspense.

The people you see in soaps aren't real; they are caricatures.

Soaps are fun to watch because they are full of action.

Soap characters are always having a crisis about something.

Stories in soaps are predictable.

Real people lead happier lives than people in soaps.

The best film ever

Ask the children what is the best film they have ever seen. Encourage them to think about such things as the storyline, special effects, dramatic moments and the performances of the actors. Then ask them to discuss their choices in groups, making sure that they share their views, to see if they agree or if others in their group have a different point of view. Stress that agreement is not necessary, but that open sharing of opinions and ideas is the aim. Ask groups to explain which film they chose and why; ask for their evaluation of their discussion.

Music

Ask children to discuss *Talking points: Music* with their group, sharing all ideas and encouraging one another to talk. Ask them to think which talking point they want to talk about to the whole class.

In whole-class discussion, bring out points about how we learn from, and about, one another, through talk.

Talking points: Music

Only people whose families play instruments, learn to play themselves.

Music can cheer you up.

Most music is really boring.

It's more fun playing music than listening to it.

Adults listen to music that children don't like.

It's easier to remember things if you make up a song about it.

Joining in with a chorus is embarrassing.

Girls like music better than boys do.

Everyone can sing.

Birds sing so they must think in music.

Where would you go?
Ask children to imagine they have been offered a two-week trip to whichever country they choose. In groups, talk about the countries or places, sharing ideas about their advantages as a destination. Ask the group to decide who has shared interesting ideas, who gave the best reasons, and what countries class members have actually visited.

What makes a good leader?
Ask the children in groups to discuss what they think are the qualities of a good leader. This can be in context, for example, a sports team leader or a group leader for a school trip. Ask them to suggest qualities they might consider important, such as courage, firmness, self-confidence, willingness to listen, ability to communicate, strength of character, sensitivity, assertiveness, tact, determination, persistence, decisiveness, calmness, intelligence, ruthlessness. Ask them to rank the qualities in order of importance, then to share their views in a class discussion.

Ask groups to suggest their ideas about who is a good leader and why. They can nominate a good leader in a range of categories, for example leader of a band, in a story or film, in politics, an admired person in sport or someone who is a role model; or they can nominate one of their own classmates.

Person of the century
Ask children to think about which historical character they would choose as 'Person of the century' (the twentieth century). Explain that ten people have been nominated: Queen Elizabeth II, Margaret Thatcher, Mother Teresa, Winston Churchill, Mahatma Gandhi, Nelson Mandela, Albert Einstein, Martin Luther King, Bill Gates, Aung San Suu Kyi.

Ask each group to research one of the nominated candidates. Explain that they will have to argue on that person's behalf even if they would not have chosen them. They must come up with at least three reasons why that person should be chosen. One of the group should present the group's reasons to the rest of the class, using persuasive language. The class can then hold a vote – or a discussion – to choose the class Person of the Century.

A five-star read
Invite children to recommend a book they have read as a 'five-star read'. Encourage them to think about the type of story and to talk about what they liked about the characters, the setting and the storyline, without giving away too much about the plot and how the story ends. Ask them to choose a short passage which they found funny or exciting and to end their recommendation by reading it.

Ask groups to share opinions using appropriate language. Ask them to be able to explain one another's point of view to the whole class.

Book of the year
Compile a short list of about four books that the children are familiar with. Invite the children in groups to imagine that they are the panel of judges who have to choose the 'Book of the year'. Discuss the things they will be looking for and ask them to agree a list of the features that the winning book should have, such as a good plot, interesting characters, suspense, a surprise twist, a moral, a story that moves the reader in some way, great pictures. Ask each group to discuss their opinions and decide together on one book to recommend; then they share their ideas and reasoning with the whole class.

If I were in charge
Ask children in groups to imagine/discuss scenarios such as these.

They are Head Teacher; they must explain three things they would change about their school and why.

They are the Prime Minister; they must explain three laws they would change or introduce and why.

They are the local mayor; they must explain three changes they would make to the local area and why.

They are the park keeper; they must explain three changes they would make to the park and why.

They are responsible for deciding on the school curriculum on Fridays; they must make three suggestions and say why their ideas are educational.

A question of manners

Ask children what they think 'good manners' means. Talk about manners with them in terms of acting in ways that display respect, care and consideration for others. Ask them to give examples of good manners and why they matter in school; and to consider if everyone agrees on the same 'manners'.

Ask groups to share their opinions by deciding if they agree or disagree with the statements in *Talking points: Manners*, and why.

Talking points: Manners

You should always congratulate winners even when you've just been beaten.

Young people should give up their seats on a bus to an adult who is standing.

You should not swear in front of your grandparents.

People should take their shoes off before going into someone's house.

You should always hold a door open for others.

It is alright for footballers to spit because they are sports players.

It is bad manners to speak when eating a mouthful of food.

You should always say 'sorry' if someone bumps into you.

Never interrupt when someone else is speaking.

It's bad manners to eat while you are walking on the street.

You should not use your mobile at meal times.

Opinions, argument and persuasion

Our ideal school
Ask the children in groups to discuss what their ideal school would be like. Encourage them to think about such things as buildings, playground and playing fields, classroom equipment, computers, space, outings, how the day would be organised, the curriculum, what breaks and what meals would be provided. Discuss opinions and decide on three important ideas to present to the rest of the class. Ask groups how easy it was to share opinions, and what strategies they employed if their group could not agree with one another's point of view.

Accents and dialects
Explain the difference between an accent and a dialect, and tell children what Standard English is. A person's accent is the way they pronounce the words they speak, which may be determined by the geographical area they come from. A dialect is the form of language with its own vocabulary and grammar spoken by a particular group or in a particular geographical area. Standard English is the form of language accepted as 'usual' in an English-speaking country. There may be serious disagreement about what this normality actually constitutes. The term 'Standard English' can be used to refer to the English spoken by those in power or those who feel they guard the history of oral language.

Using *Talking points: How we talk*, ask the children to think about whether they agree or disagree with the statements or are unsure, then to share their views in a group discussion, followed by a class discussion.

Curriculum activities and games

💬 Talking points: How we talk

You can tell where a person comes from by the way they speak.

People who speak a dialect are uneducated.

You won't get a job unless you speak Standard English.

Some accents are more pleasant to listen to than others.

It is wrong to make fun of people's accents.

Standard English can be spoken with any accent.

American accents are ugly.

People who speak a dialect are difficult to understand.

You can change your accent if you want.

People who speak dialects should be proud of their dialect.

Standard English speakers are posh.

Everyone has an accent.

People are prejudiced against anyone who speaks a dialect.

You can tell what a person is like by the way they speak.

DEVELOPING AN ARGUMENT

An argument is an exchange of views with reasons; there is a distinction to be made between 'having an argument' (a row) and a logical, considered argument that helps to establish the reasons why something is as it is. Argument may be based on premises; these underlie the reasons given and, if not sound, can make the entire argument unfounded. Provide children with examples of argument with reasons, and with the language they need to put forward their own arguments; for example teach the meaning of words such as *premise, conclusion, argument, for and against, logical, reason, agreement, disagreement.*

Ideas for practice in argument

The next activities are for practising the skills and structures of argument. Ensure that the children understand the aims for their talk, and that there is plenty of plenary time to discuss the impact and quality of talk.

Which is the most important?

Ask groups to imagine that they are the editorial team responsible for choosing the news stories to put on the front page of a newspaper. Put the headlines of the ten stories (below) on the board and ask children in groups to rank them in order of importance, then to choose what is to be the lead story and which other three stories to put on the front page. Giving reasons is very important in this activity.

Headlines:

Duke opens new hospital

British cyclist wins gold

Thousands homeless after earthquake

Vaccine discovered for common cold

British film wins seven Oscars

40 vehicles in motorway pile-up

Thieves steal paintings worth millions

Baby panda born in local zoo

Terrorist plot thwarted

Who would you choose?

Explain that the group has been chosen to go on an adventure holiday, trekking in the Himalayas. There is a chance for an extra person to join the trip. There are four applicants for the vacancy;

Curriculum activities and games

their details are below, to help the group choose. The group must put forward and listen to arguments in order to decide which applicant would be best, and why.

Arran: Has no experience of climbing but is very strong and athletic. He plays rugby. Is outspoken and likes to get his own way and can be quick-tempered at times. His teachers think he would learn a lot from being a member of such a group.

Tariq: Fitness is important to him; he is good at judo. He is very popular. He is on the school council, representing his year. Strong-minded and not afraid of a challenge. He has a tendency to be late for things. His teachers say he would fit in well.

Janila: Plays football for the south-east regional team and trains three times a week. Is doing the Duke of Edinburgh award and has done a two-day hike in the Highlands. Easy-going, but determined and likes to be put first. Her teachers say she has good leadership qualities, although she is not doing very well at school.

Tara: Hard-working, friendly and outgoing. Has been climbing before but only with her family. Her ambition is to represent Britain in the Triathlon. Can be hard to please but always makes an effort. Gets up early to train. Is highly recommended by her teachers.

About Joshua Parsons
This is a sorting activity. Provide the groups with copies of the story (below) and explain that it deals with a historical American character called Joshua Parsons. The paragraphs are in the wrong order. Ask the groups to discuss their ideas and decide on the correct order.

   A   When I asked mammy about him, she just shook her head. 'There are some things it is better you don't know,' she said.

   B   You could tell that Joshua was different. There was something about the way he looked at you and the way he held himself.

C Joshua was strong and tough. During the day the overseers kept a close eye on him as he worked in the fields. But he kept his head down and kept out of trouble.

D Joshua arrived on the plantation one day when I was about seven. Where he came from nobody knew. He never spoke about his past.

E I don't know what happened to him. One morning when I woke up he was gone. But I've never forgotten him.

F There were rumours about what Joshua had done. But no one knew for sure.

G But my mammy wasn't afraid. She took him in and bathed his wounds and he found himself a place to sleep in the corner of our cabin.

H I remember the first time I saw him. He arrived on a cart. One of his eyes was closed up and there was blood trickling from a gash at the corner of his mouth.

I Joshua and mammy would talk late into the night. Joshua talked about the rights of black people, how black and white people were equal.

J It was Joshua who opened my eyes and first made me realise that how we were treated was wrong.

K They called him Joshua Parsons. Parsons wasn't his real name. Slaves took on the surnames of their owners.

Curriculum activities and games

L People kept away from Joshua. They were frightened that if they were friendly to him the overseers would pick on them. That was the way it was on plantations.

The Badger

Provide groups with a copy of the text (below) which is from John Clare's poem 'The Badger'. Explain that the poem is written in couplets and that they are in the wrong order. Ask groups to discuss and decide what the correct order is by cutting out the couplets and re-arranging them. Remind them that they will account for their choices by offering a reasoned argument in the plenary session.

A They get a forked stick to bear him down
And clap the dogs and take him to the town.

B He comes and hears – they let the strongest loose
The old fox hears the noise and drops the goose.

C He runs along and bites at all he meets:
They shout and hollo down the noisy streets.

D And put a sack within the hole and lie
Till the old grunting badger passes by

E And bait him all the day with many dogs
And laugh and shout and fright the scampering hogs

F When midnight comes a host of dogs and men
Go out and track the badger to his den

G The poacher shoots and hurries from the cry
And the old hare half-wounded buzzes by.

Shipwrecked

Ask the children to imagine the class are shipwrecked on a desert island and there are no adults with them. Ask them to discuss in groups how they would set about drawing up a set of rules for everyone to follow until they are rescued.

Points they need to consider are: Who will make the rules? Who will enforce the rules? What rules will you have to ensure personal safety? What rules will you have about property, food, water and shelter? How will the whole group make decisions? How will you settle disputes? How will you deal with people who break the rules?

Remind children that they must put forward good arguments to support their suggestions. Share group ideas in a class discussion and draw up a set of rules on which the class agrees.

Five-point plans

Ask groups to discuss what they would like to do to improve the facilities in the school, and to make a 'Five-point plan' of how to improve the school. There needs to be an emphasis on providing reasons for ideas put forward; model use of the word 'because' for the children. Choose a group member to share their plan with the rest of the class. Decide on a whole-class five-point plan. Choose a class representative to present this, and the reasoning behind it, to the School Council.

Similarly, groups could discuss a five-point plan to improve their local area, nearby park or leisure facilities. You could invite a local councillor to hear the class plan and to discuss it with them.

Choosing a charity

Ask groups to imagine that they have raised £100 from a non-uniform day and they must decide which charity to give it to. Ask them to consider the type of charity they might support and to research specific charities and what they do. For example, they might look at a charity that helps people with disabilities, or one that carries out medical research to find cures for diseases such as cancer, one that supports vulnerable children, another that looks after sick and injured animals, or one that takes supplies to disaster-hit areas or conflict zones. Encourage them to find out what their charity does and why, and to consider what might be more important about it at the present time, to provide a reason for supporting it.

Share information and reasoning in a class discussion. Ask the children to reflect on the importance of group talk in reasoning and making important decisions.

Choose an artwork
Imagine the school has been given a windfall of £100 to buy a poster or picture for the entrance hall. Provide a set of between five and ten artworks, electronically or on paper. For example, you might use postcards or the web pages of the National Gallery. Provide information about a range of artists, subjects and styles. Ask groups to talk together to decide which artwork would best suit the school's reception area, and why. Groups could go on to research and select artworks for each classroom, again giving reasons for choices. Talk with the class about the difference between personal opinion and evidence-based reasoning.

Letter of the week
Ask groups to imagine that children have been asked to write a letter to a newspaper about an issue that concerns them. The group will act as a panel of judges of a competition to decide on the winning letter. Explain that they will have to decide what features the winning letter has so that they can justify the reasons behind their choice. Prompt groups to consider which letter has the most effective opening, states its arguments most clearly, is most persuasive, supports the arguments with evidence, adopts the right tone, uses appropriate language, involves the reader and ends neatly.

Opinions, argument and persuasion

Letter 1: Uniform

I think it's stupid that in this day and age children have to wear uniform to school. My older sister looks a right wally in a blazer with a stupid tie round her neck. The teachers don't have to wear uniform so why should we? I've got a friend who went to live in France and they don't have to wear uniforms there. They say that we'd compete against each other if we had no uniform. But I bet we wouldn't. It's stupid. They should abolish it.

Letter 2: Ban Bonfire Night

It's time we stopped celebrating Guy Fawkes Day. We've abolished the death penalty, so we should stop remembering someone being executed in such a barbaric way. Everyone is horrified by terrorist attacks and Guy Fawkes was a terrorist. But that doesn't mean we have to make a guy and burn it. Besides, Bonfire Night is dangerous. Every year people get injured by fireworks. Some of them are blinded and killed. Pets and other animals are terrified.

It's time to say enough is enough. I'd like to see Bonfire Night banned.

Curriculum activities and games

Letter 3: Overpaid

It's ridiculous to pay sportsmen so much. First Division footballers get something like £200,000 a week just for kicking a football about a field. I know they give some of it away to charity, but that's not the point. Why should they be paid so much in the first place? And some sports people are millionaires. All they do is run around, it isn't even a job. They get thousands of pounds just for losing. Why give them so much, when there are people in the world who are starving? It doesn't make sense. It's like the bonuses they give to bankers. Why are people so greedy?

Letter 4: Running out of resources

It's about time we faced up to the fact that the world is running out of resources. Take oil, for example, it won't last for ever. We need to look for alternative sources of energy. We need energy that is sustainable. We should be investing more in renewable energy sources like hydro-electric schemes, wind farms and solar energy. There's plenty a family can do, like fit solar panels and get an electric car. It will save money and help the environment. It's up to us. If we're greedy and use up all the resources that there are, there won't be anything left for future generations. We need to heed the warnings and take action now, before it's too late.

Opinions, argument and persuasion

Comics
Look at a collection of comics with the children. Encourage groups to share their opinions of comics generally, of the characters, the graphic style, use of colour and use of language. Ask them to explain which is their favourite comic and why, then to share their views on comics by discussing *Talking points: Comics*. The group should share their reasons for agreeing or disagreeing with the statements, and be ready to offer rational ideas to the whole class.

Talking points: Comics

Comics are a lot more fun to read than books.

We should be allowed to read comics at school.

You can learn a lot from comics.

Comics are full of violence.

Comics are very expensive and are a waste of money.

Comics are badly written and use a lot of made-up words.

Comics encourage children to behave badly.

The only point of some comics is the 'free gift' they come with.

A graphic novel is a better kind of comic.

Comics are for people who can't read books.

The artwork in comics is really interesting.

Verbal boxing
Organise a verbal boxing match. Choose three children to act as judges and divide the rest of the class into two teams – Team A and Team B. Then choose a controversial topic, for example: 'The school day should be longer, with an 8 a.m. start and a 5 p.m. finish.'

Team A splits into groups to prepare arguments **for** a longer school day, while Team B splits into groups to prepare arguments **against** a longer day. The judges list arguments both for and against. The

Curriculum activities and games

teams then choose one person from each group to represent their team.

Each representative 'boxes' one round of two minutes. They have to take it in turns to make a statement putting forward an argument for their team's point of view. The teacher tosses a coin at the start of each round to decide who 'throws the first punch'. The judges award two points for a very strong argument, one point for a strong argument and no points for a weak argument. They declare the result at the end of each round by adding their scores together. Then the totals for each round are added together and an overall winner is declared.

Talking points: Computer games

Encourage groups to discuss their views on computer games, taking each talking point in turn and giving the reasons why they agree or disagree with it.

Playing computer games is harmless fun.

You can learn a lot from playing computer games.

Parents should restrict the time their children play games on computers.

Games manufacturers charge too much for computer games.

Computer games are addictive.

People who play computer games are boring.

Advergames should be banned.

Violence in computer games should be more strictly controlled.

Computer games encourage sexist and racist attitudes.

Playing computer games improves your reflexes.

Computer games are dangerous; they can damage your brain.

You can waste your life on computer games.

Computer games are sociable and help you get on with people.

Opinions, argument and persuasion

Talking points: Mobile phones

Encourage the children to discuss the advantages and disadvantages of mobile phones, saying why they agree or disagree with the talking points.

Mobile phones help children to develop their communication skills.

Drivers using mobile phones should lose their licences.

Mobile phones should be banned in cafes and restaurants.

Mobile phones save lives because people can get help fast.

Mobile phones are an expensive luxury.

If your mobile rings in the cinema, you should be asked to leave.

It is bad manners to use your mobile during a meal.

Children should be allowed to use their mobiles in school.

Mobiles aren't safe; they are a health risk.

Mobile phones help you to keep in touch with your family.

Mobile phones are the best way to share things with friends.

People can use mobile phones to send you nasty messages.

Overall the positive benefits of having a mobile outweigh the negatives.

Slang

Explain that slang is a particular type of language used in informal situations. Ask children for examples. This can be quite a sensitive subject; children are often quite rightly wary of sharing what is an important part of their culture, especially in a school classroom. You could try to keep this discussion objective by looking at particular sorts of slang, e.g. use the words of a book character.

Ask the children individually to give each of the statements (over) a mark out of five (5 = strongly agree, 0 = strongly disagree), then to share their views in a group discussion.

Curriculum activities and games

> ### 💬 Talking points: Slang
>
> *People use slang to fit in, and be understood by their mates.*
>
> *People who look down on slang are just old.*
>
> *There's nowt wrong with slang.*
>
> *A person who uses slang can't speak proper English.*
>
> *Speaking slang gives a group its own identity.*
>
> *Only uneducated people use slang.*
>
> *Slang is a lazy way of speaking.*
>
> *A world without slang would be boring.*
>
> *Slang is a creative use of language and makes the language more interesting.*
>
> *Everyone uses slang words and phrases.*
>
> *You should not use slang to talk to your grandparents.*
>
> *Slang should be banned in schools.*

Register
Point out that the way we speak varies according to the situation we are in. A way of speaking in a particular setting is called a 'register'. For example, ask children to think about ways of talking when they are with their friends in an informal situation; they will speak in a relaxed, chatty, conversational style. When they are in a more formal situation, such as speaking to a teacher or to a doctor, they will tend to use a different register – that is, more formal language.

Read or show the class the two accounts Darren gives of the same incident (opposite) and talk about the different language he uses. Explain that in Account A, when he is talking to his friend, he uses informal language, including some slang terms; and in Account B, when he is talking to his teacher, he uses a more formal register.

Opinions, argument and persuasion

The incident: Account A

We were playing footie. Biggsy gave the ball a right whack. It smacked against the tree and whizzed straight through the window of Jacko's classroom. We all scarpered 'cause we knew Jacko'd do 'is nut.

The incident: Account B

We were playing football and Johnny Biggs kicked the ball so hard that it bounced off the tree and went straight through Mr Jackson's classroom window. We knew he'd be very angry, so we ran off.

Informal or formal register?
Ask the children in pairs to choose a setting (examples are given below), and decide whether the register of language will be informal or formal. Ask them to role play the scenario, then invite pairs to perform their role plays to the rest of the class. Discuss how we use different registers of talk.

Two children talk about an incident in which one of them was hurt.

A child answers a visitor's questions about their school.

A child and their friend go to the local shop together to buy ice cream.

There is an argument between two children about who has to put equipment away.

A young person explains to a councillor what she thinks should be done to improve the local area.

A young person tells a police officer about a robbery he witnessed.

Two football fans argue about which team they think is the best.

Curriculum activities and games

A teacher asks a child to explain why they have not done homework.

A parent asks a child to explain why they have not done homework.

A child asks a friend to explain why they have not done homework.

Someone asks a child to give up their seat on the bus.

The wrong register
Discuss with the class how the talk register a person uses often depends on what job they are doing. Think about the register the following people use:

A waiter in a restaurant

A newsreader on TV

A disc jockey

A chat show host

An army officer shouting instructions

A football commentator

A lawyer in court

Neighbours chatting

Builders talking to each other

A head teacher talking to a parent at a parent's evening

A nurse reassuring a patient

A shop assistant serving a customer at a checkout

Make a set of cards with the above phrases written on them. Children take it in turns to draw a card from a box. After rehearsal with their group, the child gives two examples of the person speaking – one in the correct register the person would use, and one which is obviously the wrong register.

PERSUADING AND DEBATING

The activities in this unit offer opportunities for using talk to persuade in discussions and debates. The language of persuasion is often used in written texts, but is also useful in talk.

Model appropriate language structures and find examples of persuasion in stories. Provide direct teaching of the use of persuasive language and techniques such as rhetorical questions, or actual questioning, emotional appeal or lists of three things. It is important to show children that persuasion can be misapplied to try to convince others that opinion is evidence, or can be used to try to make people do things they really don't want to. Evaluating persuasive language and techniques should not be a way of learning to be duplicitous, but a way of 'seeing through' what may be attempts to misuse persuasion.

What makes a persuasive argument in a debate?

Encourage pupils to think critically about the arguments that are expressed during a debate. Invite groups to rank the following ways of presenting an argument in order 1 to 11, with the best being 1.

The most effective way of presenting an argument is:

By saying why you hold your point of view.

By dismissing the other side's arguments as not worth considering.

By trying to make fun of the people arguing against you.

By listening carefully to what the other side says and saying why you disagree with the points they make.

By quoting other people and officials from organisations that campaign for your viewpoint.

By appealing to the audience to support your views.

By sticking to your prepared arguments.

By showing how strongly you feel about the issue.

By picking up points that other people make supporting your view and repeating them.

By quoting facts and statistics that prove your points.

By giving evidence of your own experience to support your viewpoint.

When the groups have decided on an order, ask them to share their views with the rest of the class and then hold a class discussion about the best ways of presenting arguments.

Vote for me
Ask the children to imagine that the animals in a zoo are angry. They are holding a meeting to choose a representative; they want to protest to the zoo's owners about the awful conditions in the zoo. Ask groups to decide which animal they think would best present persuasive views, then to imagine they are that animal and to create a speech saying why the other animals should vote for them. Stress the need for reasoning and the use of humour in this task. Share the speeches and analyse the persuasive approach used. Discuss the importance of group talk in creating the speech.

A charitable appeal

Ask the children in groups to imagine that they work for a charity and have been given the task of planning a 30-second TV appeal for donations to the charity. Ask them to decide what the charity is by discussing their ideas in a group. Ask the groups to then plan the appeal. They can research what makes an effective or persuasive advertisement; stress the need for accuracy and honesty. Ensure that the children use persuasive language appropriately. Role play or record the appeals. Show to the rest of the class; analyse appeals in terms of their effectiveness and their integrity.

For sale – A Roman villa

Children work in pairs or groups to imagine that they are estate agents and they have to prepare an advert offering a Roman villa for sale. Encourage them to discuss details such as the location of the building, the rooms and facilities, safety features, views and anything else in the neighbourhood that make it attractive to a potential buyer. They can then role play scenes in which one of them tells a potential buyer about the property. Record the adverts to share with the class.

Similarly, they can offer for sale a Norman castle, a medieval monastery or a Tudor manor house.

Selling the school

Ask the children to imagine that they are estate agents who have been contracted to sell the school. Decide what you think the school buildings could be used for. Would they make a good prison? A hospital? An old people's home? A warehouse? A factory? A housing development? When they have decided what they could be used for, ask them to plan how they are going to make them seem attractive to a potential buyer. Encourage them to record and share their presentation in which they use persuasion effectively, to sell the school. Ask groups to reflect on and evaluate their group work, and to highlight any problems, bringing them to the whole class for discussion and a decision about how to proceed. Ask for examples of effective group work.

Children and the law
Invite groups to discuss the age at which they think children should be allowed to do certain things. At what age do they think children should be allowed to drive? How old do they think they should be before being left home alone, or allowed to babysit for a friend? To help put petrol in a car? To have a bank account and a credit card? To walk to school alone? To leave home and live on their own? To join the armed forces? To buy and drink alcohol? To buy tobacco? To decide who to live with if their parents separate? To own a pet? To vote in elections? Encourage the children to find out what the law is about the ages at which children are allowed to do such things as to drive a car and to drink alcohol. They share their views in a group discussion, before preparing a speech for a debate in which they will express their opinion. Evaluate the quality and scope of the arguments presented, and the language used.

The holiday of a lifetime
Invite the children to imagine that a holiday company is running a competition for which the first prize is a holiday worth £5,000 for a child accompanied by a parent or carer. Entrants have to give a talk of not more than five minutes explaining where they would go and what they would do there in order to try to persuade the judges to award them the prize. It is interesting to ask children to undertake this task as individuals, then as groups, to note the difference that group discussion can make.

Studying advertisements
For this activity, you need a number of adverts from magazines. Ask children in pairs to study their advert and then to explain to the rest of the class how the advertiser tries to sell that particular product or service.

You may want to provide some questions to help discussion:

> What is in the background?

> Who is/are the subjects? Do they have personality?

> What are they doing?

What clothes are they wearing?

How is the picture lit?

What colours are used?

What props are used?

What is in the very centre of the picture?

Are there any contrasts in the picture?

What time of day is it?

How is language used; is it effective?

What emotions do you feel when you look at the picture?

What catches your eye?

On a five-star scale, how would you rate the advertisement?

Selling an idea for a product
Ask the children in groups to come up with an idea for a new product that they think will be successful, such as a spray to put on spectacles that will keep them clean at all times, or a talking walking stick that tells partially sighted people about obstacles. Encourage them to be as inventive and imaginative as they like and to prepare a detailed presentation, which includes what they consider to be the unique selling point of the product. Then ask them to imagine that they are invited to take part in a TV programme like *Dragons' Den* in which they present their idea and ask the entrepreneurs for a start-up investment of £50,000. Other members of the class can play the parts of the 'dragons' and groups can take turns at presenting their idea.

Advertising a product

Invite groups to imagine they have been asked to prepare a 30-second TV advert for a new breakfast cereal, a new fizzy drink or a new healthcare product.

Ask them to choose a name for the product and to decide on an age group who will be targets for their advert. Encourage them to discuss the image of the product that they will want to convey and to think of a slogan to use in the advert.

You may want the groups to consider various aspects of their advert:

Is the advert going to focus on the product or is it going to tell a story?

Are people going to be included in the advert? If so, what are they like and what are they doing?

Will the people speak or will you use a voice-over?

Will there be any background music? If so, what sort of music will it be?

What information about the product do you want the advert to convey?

Ask the groups to make a PowerPoint presentation of their advertisement to present to the rest of the class and to revise it in the light of any comments that are made. They can then go on to produce the finished advert.

The theme park

Ask the children to imagine that there is to be a public meeting to discuss a proposal to build a large theme park on a piece of waste ground near where they live. Encourage the children to think about the reasons why some people might be for the proposal and the reasons some people might be against it. Then, with you or another adult acting as the chair, role play the public meeting in which they take turns to express their views on the proposal.

Points to consider:

The theme park will provide jobs.

It will bring visitors to the area and local shops will benefit.

It will create noise.

There will be more traffic, causing congestion.

It will destroy the natural habitat which the waste ground provides for various species.

The site could be used for something else which the area badly needs, for example a new school.

The only people to benefit from such a proposal will be the developers.

The developers would pay for a new roundabout which would ease traffic congestion.

The value of the houses on the estate would go down.

The area is short of leisure facilities for young people.

It will cause more pollution.

Making a speech

The aim of a speech may be to inform, to entertain or to persuade. Children need to acquire the skills both of structuring and of delivering a persuasive speech.

These are some points children need to bear in mind when structuring a speech:

- Open the speech with a beginning that catches the audience's attention. One way of doing this is to begin with a question. For example, 'Why do people think it's OK to drop litter?'

- Back up arguments with evidence in the form of facts and statistics. For example, 'Ninety per cent of smokers over the age of 30 would like to stop.'
- Make statements in lists of three; this is more likely to hold the audience's attention and to stick in their minds. For example, 'People who start to gamble at an early age are more likely to end up addicted, penniless and homeless.'
- Refer to personal experiences. For example, 'I know what it is like to be bullied,' or 'I've seen pictures of houses that have been bombed.'
- Include questions for dramatic effect. For example, 'Isn't it obvious that recycling is better than throwing things away?'
- Involve the audience directly: 'It's up to us to protest about the conditions in which battery hens are kept.'
- End the speech on a strong note. For example, 'If we don't do something about it soon, it will be too late.'

Formal debate

Older pupils can take part in formal debates, which provide the opportunity for them to develop and present arguments in prepared speeches. Explain that what happens in a debate follows a set pattern, and use the technical vocabulary for debate, highlighted here:

1. The **chair** opens the debate by stating the **motion** – the topic for discussion, which is expressed formally, e.g. *'This house believes that children should be able to wear what they like to school.'*

2. Then the chair introduces the **proposer** and the **opposer**.

3. The proposer speaks first and says why they support the motion.

4. The opposer gives a speech against the motion.

5. A **seconder** for the proposer argues in favour of the motion.

6. A seconder for the opposer argues against the motion.

Opinions, argument and persuasion

7 The chair declares the motion **'open to the floor'**, which means that people in the audience get the chance to express their opinions either for or against the motion. They indicate to the chair that they wish to speak and the chair decides whose turn it is to speak.

8 Eventually, the chair stops the contributions from the audience and invites the opposer to sum up their arguments *against* the motion.

9 The proposer is invited to sum up the arguments *for* the motion.

10 The chair reads out the motion and a **vote** is taken.

11 **All those in favour** of the motion raise their hands and a count is made, then **all those against** raise their hands and are counted. Finally, all those who **abstain** (i.e. who have not voted either for or against) are counted.

12 The chair declares that the motion is either **carried**, because more people voted in favour; or **defeated**, because more people voted against.

Topics for debate

Children should be paid to come to school.

The school day should end at one o'clock.

Boxing should be banned.

Children should have to do one hour's physical exercise each day.

All forms of gambling should be made illegal.

You can tell what a person is like from their appearance.

Victims of crime should be able to decide how criminals are punished.

Children should be able to drive at 14 years old.

You should never tell a secret that you have promised to keep.

Sometimes it is better to lie than to tell the truth.

Presenting an argument – self-assessment

Is your argument developed point by point in an organised way?

Do you grab the audience's attention and involve them in what you say?

Do you quote facts and statistics to support your view?

Do you listen and respond to others?

Do you pick up points made by others in favour of your viewpoint?

Do you draw on your own experience to support your view?

Do you quote what others have said in support of your view?

Do you express how strongly you feel about the issue?

Do you pick out the main points and conclude with a summary of them?

Do you use your body language – e.g., gestures and facial expressions – to try to influence people to accept your argument?

What could you do in the future to improve your ability to present an argument?

CHAPTER 5
Conveying information

> Knowing what prompts to use has helped me speak clearly and organise my ideas. When I speak my ideas become clear in my head and then I can write them down.
>
> Naila

We use talk in our everyday lives not only to share our ideas and express our opinions, but also to convey information: we **describe** things, **recount** experiences, **report** events, give **instructions** and **explain** processes and procedures. This chapter consists of activities in which the children are provided with opportunities to develop their skills of talking to convey information. The activities provide opportunities for them to work together collaboratively as well as to prepare individual talks.

Individual talks

Children need to be taught the different skills involved in giving an informative talk. They need experience in using presentation software, and talking without such support. They need to develop their ability to refer to notes rather than to write the talk out in full; and to deliver at least some of the talk rather than reading all of it. Stress the importance of structuring the content of their talk, so that it has a clear beginning, followed by an orderly arrangement of facts and a defined – but not too abrupt – end. They also need practice in timing a talk.

Talk about trying to find an interesting way of beginning a talk, and engaging the interest of the audience. Point out that a humorous anecdote can be an effective way of beginning, but they are not always reliable!

Children will also need to develop their skills of delivery. Talk about the impression that is created by their body language, for example, and the need to stand up straight and make eye contact with the audience, including looking around the room to engage everyone.

They must also learn to project their voice so that everyone can hear them. They need to avoid the pitfall of talking too fast and realise that they can use tone of voice to stress or emphasise key facts.

Cue cards
Using cue cards in a talk or a speech enables children to make eye contact with their audience more readily. Talk about what a cue card is – a prompt to remind the speaker what comes next in their talk. Explain how to make cue cards from index or note cards, pointing out that because they are made of card rather than paper they are easier to handle.

Tips on making cue cards
The most useful cards have only one main heading or idea per card.

Use bullet points to list supporting points, ideas or examples under the main heading.

Use a highlighter to indicate where to use a slide or a visual aid.

Write on one side of the card only.

Number each card.

Write the heading in large letters so that it stands out.

DESCRIBING

Ensure that your pupils have a clear idea of what it means to 'describe' something; what sort of language you want them to use, how much detail to include, whether to use simile and imagery or to stick to the facts; and to take into account how much time is available for their descriptive talk. The children need to discuss their different points of view during drafting, and negotiate a final outcome that they are all satisfied with.

The key features of descriptive language can be used as Learning Intentions and discussed in your plenary sessions.

Key features of describing

1. Use accurate vocabulary
2. Provide effective simile, metaphor and imagery – figurative language – to help the listener to visualise, hear, touch or taste things
3. Bring something to life by portraying it clearly and enthusiastically
4. Present information in an orderly and logical sequence
5. Check for understanding in the listener
6. Be concise without leaving out important details

These are suggested activities which can give children practice in describing people and places. There will be many other opportunities to use descriptive talk in your curriculum work.

Describing a person's appearance
For this activity, you will need some pictures of different people from newspapers or magazines. Model this activity for the children, using positive description. Invite the children to work in pairs; they should look carefully at their picture. The children take it in turns to describe the person to their partner, building up a comprehensive description. You can also use portraits such as those found on the National Portrait Gallery website.

Describing costumes

Ask the children to imagine that their class is putting on a play set in Tudor times. Research what clothes people wore, then describe the costumes that Tudor people might wear in a play. Ask groups to research how clothing changed over the centuries. Ask groups to choose a time period, for example Victorian, Edwardian, the Sixties and prepare a presentation with oral description to share with the class.

Describing aliens

Ask the children to work in pairs, looking at a picture of an alien from a TV show, book or comic. They can take it in turns to describe the aliens in their picture. The pair can then collaborate to draw their own pictures of an alien, and describe their alien to the class.

Seasonal scenes

Use pictures which show one season, or the same setting in contrasting seasons. Ask groups to decide on key features and colours, phrasing their descriptive ideas as sentences or a poem. Share their descriptions with the class.

Designing a stage set

Ask the children in groups to imagine that they are responsible for designing a stage set for a play. The play takes place in one of the following contexts:

> a dentist's waiting room, a classroom, a hotel reception area, a sitting room, a kitchen, an office, a hairdresser's/barber's, a library.

Ask the groups to make sketches of the set, before explaining their ideas to other groups. They must consider what level of detail is appropriate, and also have some idea of how actors might interact with the stage set and its props.

Alternatively, pairs can imagine they have been asked to design:

> the interior of an alien spacecraft for a film, a Victorian drawing room, the hall of a castle, the parlour of a coaching inn, the living room of a medieval cottage.

The birthday present
Ask the children to imagine they are given the chance to ride in the engine of a steam train as a birthday present. They can research what a steam engine is like, before describing it to a partner.

The holiday hotel
Invite the children to imagine that they have won a competition and been to stay in a luxury hotel. Ask them to give a talk describing the hotel, its location, and its facilities such as swimming pools, games room, tennis courts and water sports centre. Encourage them to prepare cue cards referring to its different features. They could look at some holiday brochures or details of hotels online to help them prepare their talks.

A perfect place to live
Invite the children in pairs to share their ideas of what their perfect home would be like. Encourage them to think about what the building would be like inside. Ask them to focus on one particular room, such as a bedroom or living room, and to tell their partner how they would furnish it and decorate it. Ask them to think about the rooms they would have in their ideal home. Would they have a games room, a gym, or a cinema? Perhaps a swimming pool, an underground den a tree house? Where would their house be: by the beach, in the mountains, in a forest? What would the garden be like?

Ask the children individually to prepare a talk or a PowerPoint presentation in which they describe a day in their ideal home.

Describing a picture of a place
This is an activity for pairs. Explain that you are going to show a picture of a place, for example, a harbour or a farmyard. They will have 30 seconds to look at the picture, then one of them will have to describe it to their partner. After the person has finished their description, the listener can point out any details that they noticed which the person did not include in their description. Then show them another picture and this time ask the other person to give the description.

In their pairs, give one person a picture of a place, ensuring that their partner does not see it. The person with the picture has to give a description of it to their partner. When they have finished, the partner must describe the picture. The person who is the listener cannot take notes and must rely on listening carefully to the description.

Describing your home
Ask the children in groups to describe their homes as they would describe them to someone from another country. Encourage them to make cue cards and to include details of the street and neighbourhood in which they live, as well as the type of building and details of the various rooms and what each room contains. Alternatively, ask childre
n to describe a favourite shop, museum, sports venue, cinema or a relative's home. Allow scope for description of places by those who may prefer not to describe their own home.

Our classroom
Ask children to look around the classroom, noting details of the building, the furniture, the equipment, storage, colours, displays and so on. In groups, look at the school hall or another classroom. Take turns to offer a sentence about the room, using descriptive language such as adjectives and similes. Ask for a closely described level of detail. Back in class, draw and annotate a bird's-eye plan of the room, working together to agree on details.

Visit another classroom and describe this by contrasting and comparing it with their own classroom.

RECOUNTING

This section has activities which involve children in recounting experiences and events, together and individually. Children need direct tuition in how to use talk effectively to recount experiences, to report events and to present the results of investigations. It is also crucial to plan time for the children to practise the skills, and chances for them to reflect on their own competence and to provide positive feedback for classmates.

Recounting – 'telling again' – involves telling someone about a particular event or experience: saying what happened, or sharing it through talk. Recounting can be accurate or unreliable, and is always dependent on the narrator's point of view. Recounting ought to aim to be factual, but stories are often thought of as a type of recounting. The child needs to learn that there are ways to recount things that are more, or less, reliable; why it is important to be reliable; and when it is fine to tell stories.

Key features of recounting

1 Use the first person, in past tense, with clear description
2 Set the context
3 Order the events accurately
4 Include appropriate detail
5 Give reliable factual information
6 Hold the interest of the listener

Model each of the key skills for the children, or ask them to devise role plays in which they show the feature (e.g. clear description) and then its opposite (muddled description). Find examples of effective recounts, or unreliable recounts, in stories. Ask children to consider why it is important to be accurate and honest. Use a 'crime scene' scenario in which one group plays a brief scene, and the rest of the class are witnesses; ask them to recount what they saw/heard in their groups, and then consider the discrepancies.

Reflect on and discuss the overlap between recounting and narrative, and the differences. A well-known education website offers this advice for teaching children how to write recount texts: 'Try to help the reader to imagine how you felt by exaggerating your emotions and using amazing adjectives.' Given this sort of advice, it is crucial that children discuss and understand the difference between recount and story.

The key features can be used as talk Learning Intentions for your curriculum lessons.

A day to remember
Ask the children to think of a day that they will never forget because it was memorable for some pleasant reason, such as:

> a day when a baby brother or sister was born

> the day they moved house

> a day when they or a member of the family passed a test or exam

> a day when someone won a competition

> a day when they went to a wedding, birthday or family celebration.

If you feel that it is appropriate, you could ask children to recall a day when something sad or upsetting happened, such as:

> a day when someone had an accident

> a day when a pet was ill or hurt

> a day when they or a family member had to go into hospital

> a day when there was bad news.

Invite children to tell their group, and then the class, about what happened that day and why it was a day to remember. Ask classmates to provide positive feedback on the recounting style, and positive support for the context.

The big day
Ask the children to think of an example of an outing, for example:

a trip to a theme park, the seaside or water park

a weekend holiday or family outing

a shopping trip or visit to a music or sports event.

Alternatively, it could be a longer holiday or when they went abroad.

Ask them to prepare to recount their experiences. They will need to discuss with their group what is relevant, interesting and good to share, and decide on the level of detail they will offer. Encourage them to prepare the talk thoroughly and to use cue cards. Help them to plan the talk so that it isn't simply a chronological account. They might choose to talk about the most amusing incident, the most exciting incident, the most embarrassing incident, the worst thing that happened and the best thing that happened, not necessarily in the order in which they happened. They could develop the talk as a PowerPoint presentation using photos and postcards as visual aids. Share with the class or a wider audience. Ask children to evaluate their own recount in line with the Learning Intentions, and ask classmates for positive feedback and suggestions for development.

A magical day
Invite the children to imagine they spent a day in a fantasy world. They might want to think of being a magician's apprentice or flying on a dragon's back; being stranded on a planet inhabited by hostile aliens; waking up to find themselves lost in a forest or part of an animal family; riding an elephant or a unicorn; or having the ability to breathe under water or fly. Talk about their ideas with the group. Invite individuals to give an account of what happened on the magical day.

Curriculum activities and games

An incredible journey
Invite the children to imagine they went on an incredible journey, for example on a flying carpet which took them on a world tour during which they saw many famous places, such as the Eiffel Tower, the Coliseum, the Pyramids and the Taj Mahal. Encourage them to use the Internet to find out about the places that they visited and to work out the route they took, so that in their accounts they can give details of famous landmarks that they flew over, such as the Alps, as well as details of all the places they went to.

Alternatively, they can give an account of a journey into space; they could imagine they were on one of the Apollo spacecraft and give an account of the trip.

Children can imagine a trip to a European capital such as Paris, Madrid or Rome; or visits to further away places such as the Australian desert. Ask them to explain to one another what it would be like, and how they would manage the journey.

A day at a Victorian school
As part of a project on the Victorians, ask the children individually to imagine they spent a day at a Victorian school and to give an account of what they did during the day.

Two-minute talks
This is an activity designed to encourage children to 'think on their feet'. In contrast to talks which are carefully structured, this activity gives no time for preparation.

Model how to deliver an impromptu talk. Ask children to suggest a topic. Use a sand timer or a timer on the interactive whiteboard. Talk about the topic for about a minute. Then ask the class to suggest how you could continue, what details you missed out, what they would like to hear more about; or to ask questions which will encourage you to talk further. Then provide children with the same opportunity – to talk for a minute and then receive oral support and feedback in order to say a little more. Help them to work up to talking for two minutes unaided, if you feel that this length of time is appropriate for your children.

Now invite the children individually to give two-minute talks. Put slips of paper with different topics written on them into a box. They take it in turns to draw a topic from the box and then have to give a two-minute talk about it.

The topics you put in the box can be random ones ranging, for example, from pets to fairgrounds, hairstyles or the planets; or they can be linked to the topic you are studying. For example, if you are studying transport, you could give topics such as railways, aeroplanes, ships, cars, bicycles, canals, helicopters, hovercraft and motorways.

Alternatively, you could focus on favourite things, such as my favourite sport, my favourite film, my favourite game, my favourite month. Encourage children to give reasons to explain why these particular things are their favourites, to elaborate on ideas that come to mind and to describe key aspects in some detail.

Once children can talk fluently and unaided for a minute or two, ask them to consider their audience; how they will begin and end their talk; and how they deliver it in terms of tone of voice, content and structure.

REPORTING

In an oral report, as in a written report, there are certain key facts that need to be included. A report differs from a recounted text because events and incidents need not be relayed in the order that they happened.

Curriculum activities and games

> **Key features of reporting**
>
> 1 Who was involved in the event or incident
> 2 What actually happened
> 3 Where it happened
> 4 When it happened
> 5 Why it happened and what were the outcomes

Each of these key features needs to be made explicit to the children, with examples to help them seem a little less abstract. It's also important that children know why reporting is useful, and that they recognise the need for accuracy and a good level of detail.

The following activities are suggestions; you will have relevant curriculum topics for reporting. Oral reporting is a useful skill and can help children to identify the important details among all the others and subsequently to put together an effective piece of writing. Children need to learn the appropriate language for reporting, and also need chances to evaluate both their own reporting and that of classmates. You will want to teach them how to refer to facts, diagrams, pictures, graphs and evidence. Presentation software is invaluable for sharing reports using such resources, once groups have discussed what they are going to talk about, in what order, and why.

You can teach and model the skills for reporting: description and presentation. Check that children know what sort of information to present, and how to present it; how to time their talks; and how to engage with a listening audience. Make sure that in every group that presents to the class, every child speaks. Ask the audience to provide positive feedback to each group, commenting on who did what well, tones of voice, clarity of speech or information, who was interesting, informative or easy to listen to. Ask them what they have learned about the topic, and how to present a report.

In the news today
This is an activity that can be used towards the end of the day. Ask the children to imagine they are TV news reporters. Their task is to give a short report of an event that has happened at school that day. It can be something quite ordinary, such as an announcement in assembly, an incident in the playground, an interruption to a lesson, an interesting part of a lesson; or it can be something unusual, such as a talk from a visitor or a visit from a theatre group.

Decide if the report is going to be humorous or 'straight'. Ask groups to practise their talk, making sure that everyone has a chance to speak. Perhaps one group could be reporters for a whole week, then pass the turn on to the next group until the whole class has had a turn.

In today's paper
A similar activity can be developed around national or local news. Children can look online to discover what events have made today's news in national or local newspapers. They can then give a short oral report of an event that is in the news, and be prepared to ask questions about it. Again, ensure that every child has a turn to prepare and talk as reporter.

I was there
Children can imagine they eyewitnessed a significant historical event and give a report on it. The event might be a famous battle, such as the Battle of Hastings or the D-Day Landings, the signing of the Magna Carta or the Fire of London. Similarly, they could report on the assassination of Thomas à Becket, or talk about London during the great plague. Provide topics for the class to prepare, then organise a 'speech time' in which the oral reports are presented.

Nursery rhyme reports
Invite the children to imagine that they are TV reporters sent to report on an event such as Jack and Jill falling down the hill, the cow jumping over the moon or the theft of a pig by Tom the piper's son. They could work in pairs with one of them being the reporter and the other an eyewitness.

Curriculum activities and games

Reporting investigations

The following activities suggest ways in which children can present information that they have learned while researching a topic. Often this involves taking on a role. For example, you can invite children who have been studying Norman castles to imagine that they are a tour guide who is pointing out the main features of the castle to a group of tourists. Alternatively, one of the children can be hot-seated as a Norman soldier and can be questioned about what life is like in the castle. Other activities invite children to work in pairs or groups to role play situations that enable them to convey the information they have learned. For example, instead of an individual being hot-seated as a Norman soldier, a group of Normans can discuss what life is like in the castle.

Children can usefully work in groups to devise an interesting report based on their science investigations, Design and Technology design sessions, art work or music composition sessions. Reports of creative work are always interesting because creativity offers surprises and 'something new'.

The time traveller

Invite the children to imagine that they have travelled back in time to a period of history that they have been studying, such as Celtic, Egyptian, Greek or Roman times. Ask them to prepare an oral report in which they describe what life was like in those days. Ask groups to evaluate one another's reports, offering positive comments for further development.

An incredible find

Ask children either individually or in pairs to give an eyewitness account of an archaeological discovery such as Tutankhamun's tomb or the Sutton Hoo burial ship. Or they could imagine they were present when the fossilised remains of a dinosaur, such as Tyrannosaurus rex, were discovered.

A Roman soldier's life

Invite pairs to role play a scene in which a reporter interviews a Roman soldier who is stationed on Hadrian's Wall. Before they begin, encourage them to research what life was like for a Roman soldier in Britain.

Voyages of discovery
Children can discuss what they would report if travelling on a voyage round the world; for example they can interview a crew member about the conditions on board ship. Or they can be a person returning from a voyage of discovery, such as Christopher Columbus, telling his family about their trip.

A Victorian childhood
As part of a study of Victorian Britain, ask the children in pairs to role play a scene in which they discuss what their lives are like – one of them could be a factory worker or work down a mine, the other could be a chimney sweep or street urchin.

News from the front
Show pupils studying the First World War pictures of soldiers in the trenches. Ask pairs to role play scenes in which a reporter interviews soldiers and asks them what life is like in the trenches.

Evacuees
Role play a scene in which two children who are evacuees from a city during the Second World War talk about their experiences, for example of their journey, of what they were able to take with them, of their new home and school, of missing their family and friends.

Volcanoes and other natural disasters
Invite the pupils to prepare a presentation on volcanoes. This could include: an interview with a scientist who explains what a volcano is and where they are found; eyewitness accounts of eruptions such as Vesuvius, Mount St Helens, Krakatoa; a report from Pompeii describing what it is like today.

Where to go and what to see
When working on the local environment, children can produce a talk giving information for visitors about where to go and what to see in their locality. They can produce a PowerPoint presentation describing local landmarks and places of interest. Alternatively,

pairs can role play a scene in which a tourist visits a local information centre to find out about places of interest in the local area.

Dinosaurs
As part of a topic on dinosaurs, individuals can choose a particular dinosaur and use the Internet to research it, then present their findings in a talk to the rest of the class.

EXPLAINING

Teach and model effective ways of giving explanations. For example, talk about how you get to school, and the reasons for your choice of transport – car drive, walk, bus or bike ride – and the advantages and disadvantages. Give as much detail as makes your choice clear and well explained.

Key features of explaining

1 Consider what to say, in what order
2 Use concise, clear language and the correct technical terms or vocabulary
3 Sequence the explanation so that it is logical
4 Be able to answer questions to clarify details

The key features can be your talk Learning Intentions for curriculum work. Arrange for children to practise giving an explanation with a partner or group before asking them to present to the class; make sure that they know the criteria for assessment and ensure that peer feedback stays focused on this. Ask the 'audience' to provide positive feedback to each group, commenting on who gave a clear explanation; accurate vocabulary, clarity of speech or information, who was interesting or easy to listen to; and what they have learned about the topic – and how to present an explanation.

The key

In this game, children take it in turn to imagine they are a key. They explain not only what they will open but what secrets they will reveal and who they belong to. Tap into their imagination by brainstorming with the class what they might be the key to, for example a dungeon, a treasure chest, a castle door, a wardrobe, a safe, a trapdoor, a padlock on a trunk.

What makes a clock happy?

In this game, the children have to imagine that objects have feelings and to explain what makes them happy or sad. For example, a clock is happy when someone looks at it to check the time and feels sad when its battery runs down or it is shut away in an attic at the bottom of a box. Encourage the children to think of objects by looking round the classroom or visualising objects in their homes or in shops. They could be anything at all – from a light bulb to a ruler, a basket or a nail.

How to play the game

Ask the children in pairs to take it in turns to explain the object of a simple board game such as Snakes and Ladders or Draughts, or a card game such as Beggar My Neighbour, and what you have to do to win. Then, repeat the activity with them taking it in turns to explain how a computer game is played.

The rules of the game

This is an activity for individuals, pairs or groups. Invite the children to choose a sport and to try to explain how it is played to someone who has no knowledge of it. Point out that they will need to begin by explaining what the object of the game is and that they will need to explain any words or phrases they introduce which are part of the jargon – the specialised language used when talking or writing about that sport. For example, they would need to explain what a 'foul' is in football, a 'let' is in tennis or an 'over' is in cricket.

Ask the children to think carefully about the order in which they explain the rules, being careful to explain new terms whenever they are introduced. For example, they will need to explain what the goal is in football, in order to explain that the object of the game is to kick the ball over the goal-line. Encourage them to use cue cards to plan their talks.

An alien comes to school
In this activity, children imagine that an alien has come to visit the school. The alien has no concept of what a school is as they don't have schools where he comes from. In pairs, children role play a scene in which one child tries to explain what a school is, what a teacher is, what lessons are, what subjects they study, what assembly and playtime are, what happens in the dinner hour and how long the school day is. The alien should interrupt and ask questions whenever they do not understand anything.

The Countryside Code
Discuss with the class what the Countryside Code is and encourage them to use the Internet to find out about it. Talk about each rule and the reasons for it. Then invite children to role play a scene in which a farmer talks to a boy or girl who has broken one of the rules of behaviour and explains to them why it is important to observe the code.

I am an eye
As part of their work on the human body, invite children to imagine that they are a particular part of the body and to give a talk explaining what they are and what they do. Begin by getting them to work in pairs or groups, taking it in turns to be, for example, a lung, a heart, a brain, an eye, a muscle. Then ask some individuals to present their explanations to the whole class.

INSTRUCTING

Oral instructions vary from saying how to *use* something (e.g. a kettle), saying how to *make* something (e.g. bake a cake, using a recipe), or saying how to *do* something (e.g. change a bicycle tyre; or play a game).

Conveying information

Key features of instructing

1 Use the imperative form of verbs ('Do this...')
2 Sequence the statements, which should be followed in order
3 Remind the listener about safety: what to *always* do, what to *never* do
4 Factual information, diagrams and graphics
5 Use concise, clear language and the correct technical terms or vocabulary

---

Model how a set of instructions is given. Choose a scenario such as using a can opener, putting batteries in a torch, knitting a scarf, cutting fingernails using scissors – something that seems obvious but that can be broken down into steps and explained. Give instructions, leaving out key information such as keeping the can the right way up. Ask children to consider what is said, in what order. Ensure that they understand the need for concise, clear language and the use of correct technical terms or vocabulary.

Make the children aware of how a set of instructions is structured and presented. The precise nature of the instructions may vary, for example some instructions may be entirely in picture form (e.g. for toys or ready-to-assemble furniture) while others are in words. However, **clear instructions usually follow a set pattern:**

- They begin with a clear statement of the aim of the instructions.
- Next, they give details of any materials that are required, such as the pieces of wood needed to make a model or the ingredients required for a recipe.
- Then they give a list of any tools or equipment that will be needed, such as sandpaper, sticking tape or a pair of scissors.
- There is then a step-by-step guide of what needs to be done. It is important to assume that people listening to the instructions have no prior knowledge of what they are being asked to do. So

instructions need to include everything that should be done, however obvious it may seem.

It is very easy to show how important instructions are, by simply missing out some steps or using very difficult language, or making the instructions complicated. Ask children to give examples of using and following instructions – or watching parents or carers do so – from their experiences of home and hobbies. Collect types of instructions and display them, with post-it notes, so that the children can annotate them to say where the language is difficult, or how they would alter them.

Arrange for children to practise giving instructions with a partner or group, before asking them to present to the class. Ask children to give simple instructions, pacing what they say and checking for understanding. Make sure that children can ask and answer relevant questions.

Ask the audience to provide positive feedback to each group, commenting on:

- who gave clear instructions
- accurate vocabulary, clarity of speech or information
- who was interesting, or easy to listen to
- what they have learned about the topic
- what they have learned about how to provide instructions.

It is often useful to use **props** when giving instructions. The audience is more likely to be able to follow instructions that are demonstrated than ones that are not. Alternatively, the children can be encouraged to make PowerPoint slides to show the various steps, and can talk through their presentation.

I am scissors
In this game children are asked to imagine they are a particular object and to provide information about themselves to the class, including instructions as to how they should be used.

Examples of objects: a piece of cutlery, some kitchen equipment, a gardening implement, an item from a toolbox, a piece of sports equipment, an item from a workshop, an item from an artist's studio.

How to tie a tie
This is an activity for groups of three, in schools where the children's uniform includes a tie. Ask two of the children to sit back-to-back. One of them (the instructor) is going to give instructions to the other (the learner) on how to tie a tie. The third person (the observer) is going to watch.

The instructor, without watching what the learner is doing, gives instructions on how to put on a tie. The learner has to imagine that they know nothing at all about how to tie a tie and must do exactly as the instructor says.

The observer listens carefully to the instructions that are given and watches what the learner does.

End the activity after three or four minutes or when the tie is successfully tied. The observer then suggests how the instructions might be improved and the instructor and learner repeat the activity.

Pet care
With children in pairs, ask one of them to give a set of instructions to the other, who is going to look after a pet for them while they are away on holiday. They should explain exactly what needs to be done to ensure that the pet is cared for properly and give instructions on feeding it, ensuring it has water to drink, keeping it clean and exercising it. In addition, they should tell them what to do if the pet falls ill. The person listening must then repeat the instructions they have been given and the pair discuss how accurately the instructions were repeated.

A spell to turn your enemy into a mouse
Ask individuals to imagine they are a witch or a wizard, who is giving instructions to an apprentice on how to make a spell that

Curriculum activities and games

will turn their enemy into a mouse. Encourage them to prepare for this activity by listing ingredients they must use and thinking about what they must say and do to make the spell work.

How to send a text message
Ask the children to work in pairs and to take it in turns to give instructions on how to send a text message, use a new app or game, or send an email on a mobile phone.

A new ball game
Invite the children in pairs to invent a new ball game and to make up the rules for it, then to give instructions to another pair explaining how the game is played.

How to play Beggar My Neighbour
For this activity you will need a pack of cards for each group. Put the children in groups. Carefully provide instructions on how to play a simple card game, such as Snap, Happy Families or Beggar My Neighbour. Some children will already know the game and will be able to help as 'experts'. Ensure that all groups are able to play the game fluently.

Find other card games such as Clock Patience, Sevens or Donkey, and organise opportunities to learn how to play. Ask children to rehearse and explain the instructions, helping one another to use them. Discuss whose instructions were easiest to follow and why.

The rendezvous
Children in pairs imagine that they are a spymaster and a spy, and can only communicate by phone. The spymaster 'rings' the spy to say that the spy is in immediate danger and giving instructions on what to do in order to escape. The spymaster tells the spy where to meet, how to travel there, where to put the secret documents when they get there, and the signal they will give to let the spy know it is safe to hand them over. The spy then repeats the instructions and the group decides how accurately they are repeated.

The route
This is a pair activity that can be used when teaching map-reading. Individually, the children should each choose two different landmarks and plan a route between them. They then take it in turns to give directions, instructing their partner to follow the route they have planned.

X marks the spot
As part of a project on pirates or maps, encourage the children to draw the map of a treasure island, on which they mark where a treasure chest is buried and the cove where they anchored the ship. In groups, invite them to take it in turns to show each other their maps and to give precise instructions as to how to find where the treasure is buried.

The day out
In pairs, children role play a scene in which one child instructs the other on the arrangements for a day out, for example to a theme park, or to go skating or to a zoo. They instruct their friend on what time to meet, where to meet, what clothes to wear, what they will be doing for lunch, what time they will be back and whether they need to bring any money with them.

How to make Fly and Spider Pie
Invite the children to imagine they are taking part in a TV cookery series called *Gruesome Grub*. Encourage them to develop a recipe to present on the programme. They can either think of a dish for themselves or produce a recipe for one of the following: Fly and Spider Pie, Bluebottle Delight, Boiled Thistles with Slug Sauce, Mouldy Sock Soup.

How to put on a toga
As part of their topic work on the Romans, the children can take turns to give instructions on how to put on a toga. Similarly, children can learn how to put on a headdress, plait hair, lace up sandals or use hooks and eyes for fastening.

Curriculum activities and games

Out-of-order charades

Put the instructions for Charades (below) on the interactive whiteboard – they are in the wrong order. Ask groups to discuss the game and how it is played, and to put the instructions in the correct order.

Instructions for charades:

If preferred, the team can mime instead of acting the syllables.

The team then act the following syllables.

A coin is tossed to decide which team goes first.

The object of the game is to guess the word that is being acted.

If they fail to guess the word, the first team choose another word.

Finally, they act out a scene in which the whole word is included.

The teams take it in turns to choose a word of two or more syllables.

The players are divided into two teams.

The team that wins the toss goes first.

They act out a scene in which they include the first syllable.

The word must divide into syllables which are words themselves or sound like words, e.g. pass–port, com–fort–able.

If the watching team guess the word, they choose the next word.

Any number of people can play the game.

CHAPTER 6
Talk across the curriculum

> Speaking helps you in every subject; you need to explore your thoughts and Mrs Townend helps us to use the correct features and what she calls 'Standard English.' This means we can use the right language in the right places at the right time and that means we can compete with the best.
>
> Mehroz

PAIRED LEARNING INTENTIONS

Learning Intentions to do with talk can usefully be twinned with LIs from any curriculum area. In this way talk activities are integrated into your classroom day. Indeed it is so important to teach children a range of talk repertoires that it is sometimes helpful to think of the curriculum as simply the set of contexts we can use to teach the all-important skills of talk! Children can be reminded to think about how they are speaking or listening, and can be asked to report back at the end of the session, evaluating how their talk helped their own learning and how they have learned from their group through talk.

You will know the strengths and weaknesses of the children in your class, and be able to decide which areas of spoken language they need you to teach and practise with them.

Learning Intentions which can help to generate exploratory talk are:

- To include everyone in the group
- To share all ideas openly

- To ask for, and give, reasons
- To challenge what others say in a respectful manner
- To sum up and come to an agreement

Each of these could, for example, be paired with all curriculum Learning Intentions for a week. After five weeks, your class will be more aware of the power of talk, and more capable of expressing their ideas and listening to others.

Importantly, this gives you the opportunity to talk about talk in your closing plenary sessions at the end of lessons. The discussion you have with children will depend on your talk objective, but, for example, you can ask such questions as 'How did your group make sure everyone was asked to talk?', 'Who listened carefully and how do you know?', 'What reasons were you given?', 'Did you all agree, and if not, how did you show this?' It is very good for children to hear that others appreciate their efforts to discuss things effectively. It gives children the chance to shine at things they did not know they were good at – for example, a child may struggle to write, but may be flagged up by their classmates as a great listener.

Your talk with children about their curriculum work ensures that there is a clear continuity between your lessons. Children need explicit links made between what came before, what we are doing now, and what we might go on to next. You can also use new vocabulary in an appropriate context, to consolidate new uses of words. Talk with children helps to support individuals as they work to make meaning, as misconceptions are aired and new points of view are presented to them.

The Learning Intentions for exploratory talk can be broken down into more achievable steps if needed. For example, *To ask for, and give, reasons* is quite a lot to do for a learner. This could be broken down into smaller steps and presented as LIs across a range of curriculum subjects, over a reasonable length of time. The steps might be:

- To ask why.
- To ask: What is your reason for what you just said?

- To listen to a reason and decide if you agree
- To listen to a reason and think of another reason why/why not
- To use 'because'
- To give a reason without being asked
- To give a reason backed up by facts, information or opinion
- To compare reasons and decide which you think is good

Example of paired Learning Intentions: Talk and Mathematics

Each of the following activities lends itself to discussion about the talk involved, in your closing plenary session. Children should be able to evaluate their own talk and that of others, and make suggestions about how to change things if they feel that they are not using talk effectively.

Topic: Two- and three-dimensional shapes

Session 1: Triangles

Talk LI: To include everyone in the group

Maths LI: To understand key facts about triangles

Group activity: Ask everyone in your group to contribute all known ideas and questions about triangles.

Session 2: Plane shapes

Talk LI: To share all ideas openly

Maths LI: To look at a range of plane shapes and identify key features

Group activity: Look at plane shapes and share all that we know about them.

Session 3: Tessellation

Talk LI: To ask for, and give, reasons

Maths LI: To understand the idea of tessellation

Group activity: Choose a shape; make a prediction with reasons, then draw round it to check for tessellation. Repeat for several shapes. Think about an explanation of why some shapes tessellate and others do not.

Session 4: Nets and 3D shapes

Talk LI: To challenge what others say in a respectful manner

Maths LI: To predict which nets will make 3D shapes

Group activity: Look at nets and decide together which will and will not make a 3D shape. Record ideas and reasons. Make shapes from the nets.

Session 5: Share about shapes

Talk LI: To sum up and come to an agreement

Maths LI: To articulate ideas using mathematical vocabulary

Group activity: Create a presentation which will teach classmates about one 2D shape, and its corresponding 3D shape(s) and tessellating patterns, within a time limit. Present to the class with all group members speaking.

Talk vocabulary for curriculum thinking

These words should be taught, talked about, displayed and commonly used in your classroom:

thinking   exploratory talk   listen   discuss   agree   disagree   reason   opinion   knowledge   information   negotiate   compromise   decide   team   collaborate   group question   hypothesise   predict   a good point/idea/reason   changed my mind   learned   unsure   don't follow   don't understand   please say more/explain/elaborate

SPECIAL OPPORTUNITIES FOR TALK ACROSS THE CURRICULUM

This section gives examples of some contexts in which spoken language is particularly valuable in particular curriculum areas, along with some of the specialised vocabulary that children need to begin to use. These are not exclusive, but simply starter ideas – you will be able to create better ideas that match what your class needs, knowing the stage that they are at and the topic you are studying.

As you are aware, it is just as important that children learn to express uncertainty about their curriculum knowledge, as it is that they share what they do know. If a child can identify what they do not know or understand, and can say so, they are in a strong position to learn.

Talk in Mathematics

Comparison, e.g. size and shape of containers

Prediction, e.g. of capacity, length, next step in a pattern

Sorting, e.g. shapes by colour, size, edges, corners, vertices, faces

Estimating, e.g. length, height or weight before measuring

Looking for patterns in numbers, using the language of reasoning

Probability

Discussing different ways to tackle a number problem

Deciding what a graph or chart tells us

Undertaking practical activities to practise key mathematical concepts

Talk in Science

Considering what is observed

Thinking up a testable question – what to investigate?

Deciding how to conduct the investigation

Creating a prediction or a hypothesis, using reasoning

Evaluating practical work as it proceeds

Working out what the evidence tells us

Communicating findings

Asking further questions

Talk in English

Predicting what is going to happen

Describing or evaluating a character

Creating a new scene, paragraph or character

Thinking about alternative endings

Considering words and phrases in a poem

Looking at rhyme, rhythm or shape in a poem

Linking story, art and music

Planning for writing

Deciding why certain words have been used

Talk in Music

Selecting a piece of music/song and preparing a dance/presentation to accompany it

Analysing and commenting on music

Considering rhythm, tone, tempo

Using music to represent ideas such as growth, change, stages of a cycle or event

Thinking about music and characters in stories

Creating a dance to music

Talk in Physical Education

Talking about following rules to make a game work

Considering relationships between members of a team

Analysing the progression of a game or sequence of actions over time

Discussing language use between team mates, and with opposing teams

Thinking about what makes a good spectator, or coach

Talk in Geography

Thinking about food production and transport

Analysing maps, routes, graphics and descriptions

Using questions to find out about artefacts

Outdoor work – planning, safety, virtual field trips

Talk in History

Thinking about chronology

Sharing understanding of the past to create a clearer picture

Enquiring into mysteries, events, people and changes

The lives of other people, especially children

Interpreting resources and thinking about artefacts

Talking about the past

Talk in Design and Technology

Deciding on a team

Identifying and establishing a problem or puzzle

Thinking about design and materials

Considering health and safety in manufacture

Evaluating design in use

Reflecting on how things appear, their surfaces or features

Talk in Religious Education

Considering religious symbolism, dress or imagery

Describing buildings and artefacts using accurate vocabulary

Asking questions to find out information, or discussing different points of view

Planning a visit to a religious site, building or ceremony

Making models, displays, puppets or cooking

Using artefacts – questioning and speculation

Talking about ideas, belief and faith

Considering a range of points of view

Talk in Art

Inspirational activities, pictures, experiences, conversations

Using visual perception in description and planning – responding to art

Planning and working at museums and galleries

Describing and evaluating work as it is in creation

Looking at colour, light, shade, tone, symbolism

Choosing artworks for particular settings and contexts

IDEAS FOR CROSS-CURRICULAR TALK

There are some useful contexts which stimulate and foster talk, allowing children to share ideas, enjoy talking to one another, and learn from and with one another. Encouraging talk by setting it in an enjoyable context can help children to practise new vocabulary, and to hear words put to use to get things done. This section suggests some contexts in which talk is the medium through which communication happens. Each of them is based on the sort of situation that the children may one day find themselves in!

Quiz show
Use the format of a TV quiz show with teams and a chairperson. The quiz can be about topic work, sport or general knowledge.

Role play
Ask children to rehearse and perform simple role plays to bring to life historical characters, to act out items in the news, or school issues such as bullying or inappropriate behaviour on the playground.

Interview
Some real posts may need to be filled – classroom helpers, liaison with other classes, recycling, taking messages. Either provide a brief interview schedule of questions, and set up your room so that children interview one another; or ask them to devise the questions. Children can suggest classmates who are persuasive or well suited to the jobs with vacancies. Interviews can also be about hobbies and pastimes, or can be a kind of role play with the interviewee in role as a book character, 'hero' or historical figure.

Demonstration
Ask children to demonstrate to others, in a group or whole class, their practical work undertaken in Science, Art or D&T. Ensure that the child has the appropriate vocabulary to explain what they did and what the outcomes were, and that they understand that in a demonstration they will be expected to explain the task and show how to do it simultaneously. Check that audience members know that they will be expected to ask a relevant and supportive question.

Presentation

Using electronic means or otherwise, ask children to prepare to present something – their ideas, a story, a poem, a picture, a series of slides – to the class. Preparation will involve group discussion and decision-making. Presentation involves using appropriate vocabulary, speaking clearly and being able to answer questions.

Trial

Set up a courtroom context to conduct a trial of a book character (as happens in *Alice in Wonderland*). This can be done entirely orally. The children will need to be aware of the character's goings-on by becoming familiar with their story. You can have a full range of courtroom characters: judge, barristers, solicitors, jury, security guards, clerks, family and friends, witnesses – and the character(s) on trial. You may also want to include expert witnesses or character witnesses who can say something about the character's mental health. Prepare by allocating roles, modelling how a court works or showing this on video, then giving time for reflection on roles. Run the trial, including allowing the jury time to consider their verdict. Have a class discussion about sentencing.

Ask children to evaluate their own role and that of others, and to try out different roles.

Most characters do something contentious in a story book, so there are plenty to put on trial. For example: Goldilocks, any 'wicked stepmother' or 'wicked witch' character, Aunt Sponge and Aunt Spiker (from *James and the Giant Peach*), Paddington, Peter Pan, Benjamin Bunny, Count Olaf (of the Lemony Snicket books), a bad wolf or fox, Voldemort, Willie Wonka, Captain Hook, Cruela de Vil. These are mainly classical stories but any contemporary work you are looking at with the children will have its wayward characters or downright villains.

In addition to these Literacy examples, a trial may be part of any topic; for example, you might set up the trial of a poverty-stricken Victorian child who has stolen a loaf of bread to take home for their family. Or a 'scientist' can be asked to account for results which they have made up; a farmer might be put on trial for running a farm in which battery hens are kept in terribly small cages. Opinions about what is right or wrong, or what rules societies run by, can be aired in mock trials in PSHE topics.

Question-and-answer session
Ask groups to research information for the topic you are studying in class. Provide a list of all the topics, and ask groups to devise a question to ask for each topic. Run the session so that each group in turn asks a question, and all group members have to contribute when it's their turn to answer. 'We don't know' is an acceptable answer and a starter for further research.

Informative talk
Invite a visitor into class. This can be a parent with an interesting story, a child who moved school, a student from the local secondary school, a new teacher, a teaching assistant from a different class, a health professional, a mum with baby, someone with a puppy and so on. Ask them to talk to the children for 15 minutes or so. Ask the children for questions for the speaker.

Political hustings
Election of School Councillors or class representatives can be an opportunity for hustings. Candidates are proposed and seconded, and have the chance to prepare what they will say to persuade others of their suitability. This can be a group task, with each group nominating a candidate after discussion, and the group representatives then going forward to the class hustings. The candidates should expect to answer questions, and the class should put supportive but probing questions to them.

After such an experience, children can evaluate their own performance and that of others, and think about the difficulties inherent in talking to a large audience.

Soap box
Ask children to think about issues or factual topics that they are genuinely interested in, and prepare to talk for one or two minutes without notes or a presentation to help. You could have a 'soap box' session once a week in which children take turns to hold the

floor and talk about their concerns. There is a lot of teaching and learning to do before some children will have the confidence, vocabulary and 'nerve' to get up and speak; others will have no problem. The idea is to give every child the chance to have a voice in the classroom, and for their classmates to respect their ideas and the way they can talk about them.

Creating a building

Architects and designers 'talk a building into existence' before creating the physical thing. There's much to consider, such as the materials, the impact on the local environment, and the client's requirements. So, there's a lot to say in the planning, design and prototyping process. Children are very keen to just get on with things without spending inordinate amounts of time sitting around a table talking; and they are right to do so. The chance to do something, evaluate it and have another go is invaluable. Using simple materials, children can go through these processes in discussion with one another. For example, provide equal amounts of dry spaghetti sticks, masking tape, modelling clay and a marshmallow for each group; ask children in groups to see who can build the tallest tower that will hold up the marshmallow. Provide a newspaper and ask them to design and make a structure to support the most weight.

It isn't necessary to be competitive; groups can design an environment for a woodlouse, or a new classroom or a better playground, with classmates appreciating and evaluating the designs rather than trying to 'win'. The focus as always should be on effective talk, respect for their own and others' ideas and attentive listening.

Business meeting

If there is a decision to be made which involves a variety of expertise, or contributions from children who have had different experiences, a business meeting can be an effective forum. Note that in a business meeting, participants are not equals as they are in exploratory groups. It is useful for children to learn that this is how some meetings are run, so that they can see how to contribute even when it may seem daunting to do so. You can usefully teach the children the difference between exploratory groups and business meeting groups.

TAKING ROLES IN A GROUP

For some tasks you may want to assign conventional roles to group members. Everyone should have the chance to take on each role at some time; ask the children to keep a record of which roles they have fulfilled, with their observations and comments on their perception of the role and themselves in it.

Model each role in advance in a whole-class setting so that children can understand what they are required to do – and not do.

Here are some roles to try.

Chair
It is the responsibility of the Chair to organise turn-taking, to direct the discussion and to time it.

An effective chairperson will:

Begin the discussion by reminding the group what the topic is

Decide whose turn it is to speak

Make sure that everyone in the group gets a chance to speak

Ensure that one person does not dominate the discussion

Keep the discussion focused on the task

Move the discussion on to the next point

Make key suggestions to keep talk flowing

See that the ground rules are observed

End the discussion

Support the reporter to summarise the group's views or decisions

Reporter

The reporter must attend to the discussion, keeping a track of key points and issues raised. They should be ready to report back to the whole class on behalf of the group; they should feel free to express their own opinion, but must not allow it to influence them unduly when giving their report. This task needs rehearsal and the support of other group members.

An effective reporter will:

Take notes of key points as they are made during the discussion

Be prepared, if there is not a consensus, to explain that different members of the group hold different opinions

Summarise the reasons given for different points of view

Quote any key evidence that has been mentioned

Explain the group's ideas concisely

Scribe/Recorder

This person is responsible for recording the discussion, a difficult task. Recording can be oral, note-taking, video or by drawing.

An effective scribe/recorder will:

Take notes or make a diagram, a video or sound recording

Ensure that they record key points fairly and accurately

Ask for clarification if necessary

Be prepared to talk about or explain their record

Time-keeper

If the Chair requests, the job of keeping time can be delegated.

An effective time-keeper will:

Ensure that they are aware of the start and end time for discussion

Listen carefully to the discussion

Check with the Chair to see what input is needed

Offer time-markers, being sensitive to the speaker

Interpreter
Children learning to speak English benefit from targeted help from a peer. This support can help children to understand what is said, and to make their own contribution.

An effective interpreter will:

Translate key words/phrases for group members when needed

Listen carefully

Interpret without interrupting or disrupting the discussion

Specialist/Researcher
Groups may need to prepare in advance if they are to discuss issues requiring specific factual information. The role of finding things out can be assigned to a group member.

An effective specialist/researcher will:

Prepare evidence or information in advance of discussion

Be prepared to contribute orally when asked

Have information sources to hand if needed

Listen carefully and contribute factual information

Critic/Observer
Groups benefit from a listener who is looking out for potential problems on behalf of the group. This should be seen as a positive role.

An effective critic/observer will:

> Listen and think about ideas and suggest problems that may arise, for example if the discussion becomes unfocused or someone starts to dominate the discussion.
>
> Offer constructive criticism which positively influences the discussion. The observer can point out when a person helps move the discussion forward either by introducing a new point, referring back to a previous point or refocusing the discussion.

Group members
Everyone, whatever role, is responsible for the effective working of the group.

An effective group member will:

> Listen carefully to others' views
>
> Signal the chairperson they wish to speak, and wait their turn to speak
>
> Avoid interrupting
>
> Stick to the topic under discussion
>
> Back up their views with reasons, wherever possible quoting facts and evidence to support their views
>
> Explain why they disagree with other people's views, referring back, where appropriate, to what has been said earlier in the discussion
>
> Ask questions to seek clarification or explanation
>
> Help the reporter to rehearse a summary

CHAPTER 7
Talk about stories, poems and drama

> I think talking time is good because I get to talk in class and I can cooperate with my group. The bad part is that I get over-excited because I like it.
>
> Thomas

TALK ABOUT STORIES

After our human needs for food, drink and shelter, we seem to need others and their stories. Stories describe events, people, places and things in imaginative and interesting ways. They often have a narrative path that we as listeners follow, wanting to know what is going to happen and perhaps imagining endings for ourselves. Stories contain surprises. They can involve a child in a way that makes them really mind very much if something goes wrong, or right, for a character. The characters can come alive and seem real. Stories can give children the chance to experience things that they never will in reality, and can encourage them to think about difficult ideas and emotions. Children can learn to become good listeners by being involved in hearing a story: they can attend, follow closely and reflect on what they hear. The chance to listen to, and tell, stories involves children in their community and its concerns. Studying the mechanics of how stories work and how to construct sentences is important, but may miss the essence – the story and the child are linked by the way language is taken into the mind and retained, remixed, reflected on and wondered about. Listening to and talking about stories is crucial; people account for themselves through story, and the child needs chances to learn how this happens and how best to do it themselves.

Oral story-telling has a long history; stories have been told to entertain, enlighten, teach and rehearse events, and particularly used as a way to talk about special characters and their lives. Long ago, all stories were told, rather than written; and even now, people like to hear and tell stories, about themselves, their communities or about other places, people and times. Computer games make full use of story, as do advertisers and journalists in print, on film and online. Story-telling involves both recounting the main narrative, and embellishing it by use of word and gesture. We all account for ourselves to others through story in an everyday way – how our day went, what a holiday was like, what we plan to do and what is going wrong. Children need to develop their oral story-telling skills, so that their account of themselves can become more purposeful, more accurate and clear; so that they can exercise their imagination; and so that as listeners they can become more discerning and more curious. Some children find it easy to talk about themselves and to imagine themselves into stories. Others find it impossibly difficult. In school we can teach some ways to tell and listen to stories that will help every child to articulate the events and emotions in their life more readily, and help them to listen to and empathise with others.

Story-telling in tradition
There are traditions in story-telling that can be made explicit, and become useful for the child as they set out to tell their own stories. The following list has examples of some story-telling devices, techniques and traditions that help listeners to make sense of a story. Listening can be difficult, so providing a link with other stories is both reassuring and enables meaning to be made. The importance of gesture, audience interaction and fluency can also be emphasised and taught. The features or structures of a good story can be directly taught.

Curriculum activities and games

Features of a good story

1 **Story vocabulary:** reassuringly familiar words can help a story along as the listener relates the story to others they have heard: 'Once upon a time', 'a beautiful princess', 'a handsome prince', 'a sly fox', 'and the very next day', 'for a year and a day', 'happily ever after' – and so on.

2 **Repetition:** repeated words or phrases and repeated events.

3 **Rule of three:** there is something catchy about 'three': three brothers set out, three wishes, three witches, three rings, a choice between three things.

4 **Journeys and quests:** characters set out and go places, finding or losing things on the way, meeting others and developing as they go.

5 **The hero:** often mistaken for someone else, or loses their identity, meets a character in need of help, is rather innocent and naive, is honest and brave, is on a quest or journey for some noble purpose, is surprising or breaks out of their stereotype.

6 **Disguises and mistakes:** characters may not know who they are, or may have been transformed or disguised, later to be discovered, may be lost or banished or have to hide, or may by their own agency be punished or rewarded. Things can be lost, forgotten or stolen; or found, remembered, returned.

7 **Learning:** stories teach and help to convey information, cultural values, and important ideas.

8 **Good and evil (and other opposites):** the impact of behaviour on others, and the way that 'the best laid plans' may be derailed by smart thinking, goodness, evil or chance.

The child's use of voice in oral story-telling

Asking children to tell their section of a story in a whole-class setting is a wonderful opportunity for the confident, and a nightmare for the quiet, shy or diffident child. It is a good idea to create equal circumstances for all. Ensure that speakers have a hand-held or lapel microphone so that voices are all of a similar volume, and the quiet child is not made even more fearful by being told to 'Speak up!' Make sure that there has been plenty of time to rehearse. Ask groups to present to just one other child, their group or to yourself or your teaching assistant before presenting to the whole class. For children who simply cannot or will not speak, ask their group mates to carry on as if the oral contribution was there – to include the child and to ensure that their name and presence are acknowledged. A confident, speaking classroom will encourage every child to see what is possible, and take the small steps they need to take in order to talk, to join in, knowing that what they say aloud will be received by a friendly and supportive audience.

Story talk and writing

It's interesting to keep an oral story alive just by having children tell versions of it over time. This is a good use of memory and recall, and, in particular, supports development of working vocabulary. Children may readily learn new words but may have no chance to use them in other contexts. Oral story-telling can provide chances to bring out vocabulary and put it to good use. The story told can be an imaginative one, or can be about a science investigation, a school journey, about lessons undertaken in history or music – anything that the child has experienced.

Oral story-telling can be the basis of subsequent writing. The skills of each are very different, and are of equal value. Not all stories have to be written down; but having had the chance to talk about a story can certainly facilitate later writing. Also, if a group has the same story in mind through having discussed it, writing becomes much more possible. Ideas can be checked and joint recall of detail can support the writing process.

Teaching story-telling

Ask groups to rehearse telling a simple story, a folk tale or story from a picture book. Each child should recount a section of the story, even if it is only a few words or something a character says. Teach children how to respond with respect and support for their classmates while listening; provide a safe and supportive classroom forum for the stories to be told. Ask groups to use their own creativity to talk about how to re-tell, embellish or alter the story.

Provide chances to practise telling sections of stories out loud. For example, ask groups to come up with a good story opener involving: the sea and a storm; a fox and a trap; someone who is lonely on their birthday; a lost pet. Ensure the groups work to prepare an opener in which every child speaks. Share stories orally with the class, asking for comments on what was interesting, for suggestions and contributions.

Ensure that the children are aware of the steps involved in telling a story; for example read a story with them and point out a good opener, character description, setting, a problem, a resolution, a neat ending. Stress the power of imagination and the need to make sure that the 'reader' (listener) understands what is happening. Talk with children about timing, repetition or any key aspects of story on which you are focusing, such as factual information, character or setting.

You will be aware of the interests and aptitudes of the children in your class. To assist children's following of a story it may be necessary to edit it, for example by cutting out unnecessary descriptions, clarifying the storyline or providing pictures which help with the text. In addition you may want to display vocabulary, characters or settings. You can use puppets or toys for key characters, or provide a full 'story sack' – a bag of resources such as the story, a jigsaw, word cards, character toys or puppets, games and DVDs – so that the children can engage with the story in a variety of ways. If children are to recount their science, maths, geography or history experience as story, then they can use equipment, pictures or diagrams and graphs, to prompt and support their account.

Story-telling in groups

In this section we suggest story-telling activities designed to be undertaken in a group, with every child contributing equally and all encouraged to take part in oral presentation. You will need to model the skills needed, and make use in plenaries of the good examples that you see happening in your talk groups. Ask effective groups to repeat their discussion for the class, or ask individuals to give an account to the class of how working in a group has helped them.

The footprints

Children take it in turns to describe a strange set of footprints that they have seen and to speculate whether the footprints belong to a person, an animal or a supernatural being. The footprints could be, for example, inside a building on a carpet, dusty floor or tiled floor, or outside along a path or in a garden. Encourage the pupils to describe where the footprints are, as well as the footprints themselves.

The box

Ask the children to work in pairs and to imagine they find a box somewhere. They take it in turns to describe the box and what they find when they open it.

Keep talking

Ask groups to give themselves a number each. Provide a picture, sound or oral story stimulus and make sure that children have heard some useful vocabulary relating to your stimulus. Child 1 begins the story and must talk for 30 seconds. Child 2 then takes over and must continue the story for another 30 seconds, after which Child 3 continues the story. The last person has to finish the story in 30 seconds.

An alternative is to remove the time constraint and ask groups for more natural 'turn taking'.

Ask groups to recall and rehearse their story for presentation to the class. Remind them that every child should speak.

Retelling a story

Read the class a well-known traditional tale and then invite them to re-tell the tale to one another in their own words. Make this more creative by asking them to embellish the story with gesture, speech, adjectives, a separate new scene or character, or a different ending. Ask groups to perform their story for the class. Groups can make a PowerPoint presentation or a set of pictures to show on the interactive whiteboard, to support and enhance their story-telling. Ask the class who are listening to highlight effective features of the story and to say what was well told, clear or interesting.

What makes a good story?
Invite the children individually to think about what are the features of a good story, and why. Ask them to rank the features (see box) on a scale of 1 to 10, in which 10 is a very important feature and 1 is unimportant. Ask groups to share their views and come to a decision, ranking the features in order. With the whole class, ask for ideas and reasons, and make some class decisions about what matters most. Ultimately the importance of these features might depend on the sort of story, the audience, whether the story is written or told and so on. However, it is useful to have such features in mind when story-telling, and this is one way to try to raise awareness and to hear other points of view.

What makes a good story?

Characters you can identify with
Detailed descriptions of the setting
A surprise twist of the plot
A story that moves you, e.g. makes you happy, sad or scared
A clear moral or message
A storyline that is easy to follow
Interesting characters who change and develop
Plenty of action
Lots of dialogue
An imaginative storyline
A satisfying ending
Ideas in the story that make you think
An original idea
A story that has animals in it
A story that is believable

Off to a good start?

In this activity groups evaluate story openers and share ideas about what is effective. The opportunity to do so can help children to start their own stories more effectively. Provide story openers on paper or on the interactive whiteboard. Ask children individually to think about the words, then to rate the sentences on a five-point scale (5 = a very good opening, 1 = an uninteresting opening). Then ask children to share their thoughts with their group, justifying their ideas, asking for and giving reasons. Ask groups to prepare for whole-class work by choosing three sentences they think are the most effective story openers, and to be ready to say why.

Story openers:

> Someone in a silver suit carrying a small parcel strides purposefully towards the door of the lift.
>
> It was a cold December day and the forecast was for snow later.
>
> As Lucy skated down the street, she felt very cross.
>
> His head ached, and as he began to wake, he realised that an unfamiliar face was peering at him.
>
> When people are happy, they all seem the same, but unhappy people are always unhappy in their own way.
>
> The door opened and an elephant appeared.
>
> As the moon drifted behind a cloud, a shadowy shape emerged from behind the wall.
>
> As the bus pulled away, they took a last look at the village.
>
> There it was again, the faint scratching noise that had woken me.
>
> The bell rang and the playground emptied.

It is a well-known fact that a black and white kitten can easily find a good home.

It was a mad idea, but there was no choice —

There was no possibility of taking a walk that day.

What happens next?
When reading a story to the class, stop at suitable points, or at the end of a chapter, and ask the children to predict what happens next. Ask them to give the reasons for their predictions. Ask groups or pairs to think together about their predictions before sharing ideas with the class. Provide a picture of a new character, and ask groups to create a description.

It is quite important to distinguish between this stop-start, teaching activity, and reading a story straight through without losing its integrity and atmosphere. There is surely time for both.

A different ending
Ask the children to focus on the ending of a story which they have been reading. In a whole-class discussion, ask them whether they found it a satisfactory ending. Did it surprise them or did they expect it? Did it have a message? Ask groups to discuss alternative endings. If there had been another chapter in the book, what would have happened in it? Ask the children to dramatise their own ending or be prepared to share it orally. Ensure that children listening to classmates are ready to provide positive and supportive feedback, and to make honest and sensible suggestions for further development of ideas.

Meet important characters
Choose one of the class to take the hot seat and act as the author of a story which the class has just read. Prepare for this activity by asking the class to think of questions they would like to ask the author about the book: for example, about the viewpoint from which it is written, the theme, the characters, the setting and the plot.

Talk about stories, poems and drama

Ask children to take the hot seat and be a famous person, for example a scientist, musician, or historical figure you are studying, and to tell their story, prompted by questions from the audience. Ensure groups have discussed questions they will ask in advance.

Choose a child to take the hot seat and be a character from a story, for example one of the three bears, a bad wolf, a lost boy, a character from a story with which your class has become familiar. Ask groups to prepare and ask questions. Make use of the questions and answers in later written work.

What if...
Choose a context to use as the start of a class story which the children can continue. Read the starter phrase aloud and ask groups to think together to decide how the story would proceed, and to be ready to share their ideas with the class.

What if...

> you woke up one morning and you found yourself inside a cage
>
> you arrived at school one day and found it wasn't there
>
> you and a friend were in a lift which stopped between floors and the door opened
>
> you were playing a computer game and became part of the game
>
> you were playing in the park when a cave suddenly appeared and you went in
>
> a spacecraft landed in the garden and you were invited in
>
> you were walking home from school when a dragon flew down and tapped you on the shoulder
>
> you came across a puppy that was hurt and found it could talk to you
>
> you wanted to talk but found you couldn't

TALK ABOUT POEMS

Oral poetry has a long and venerable history, having been used to record the events that shaped communities, their laws, religious texts, ideas and hopes. We still use poems to provide children who have not yet learned to read with ways to remember the alphabet, days of the week, numbers and so on. Poetry is characterised by having rhythm, and by its ability to say more than a literal reading of its words would indicate. Rhythm and refrain aid memory of a poem, as does a poem's facility to combine with music and become lyrics for a song. Some songs we hear as children stay with us for life; poetry and lyric are powerful uses of words. Poetry can be very memorable, from advertising jingles to history plays.

There are many forms of poetry; no doubt in the hands of a good teacher, any poetical form can be learned and read or spoken aloud. We mention three forms here, which are commonly used in classrooms because of their accessibility, their rhythm, humour and power.

Epic poetry: An epic is an extended narrative in verse, usually telling the exploits or journey of a heroic figure as they undertake amazing adventures and win through. The epic poem might use particular techniques such as repetition, alliteration or extended simile, to carry the listener along. An example is Homer's *Odyssey*. Passages of epic poetry offer fascinating story content, big characters and strong rhythm.

Narrative poetry: Narrative poetry sets out to tell a story, using rhyme and rhythm. Narrative poems may have a moral or a message about human behaviour. Examples of narrative poetry are Robert Browning's 'The Pied Piper of Hamelin', 'The Highwayman' by Alfred Noyes and 'Mending Wall' by Robert Frost.

Limerick: Limericks are humorous five-line poems with the first, second and fifth lines rhyming with one another. Limericks are memorable because of this rhyme scheme, their brevity and wit; they are surprisingly difficult to write!

What is a poem?
This question is really impossible to answer, as poets will always break out of conventional forms to create new genres. But it is useful to air ideas and see what everyone thinks. Encourage children in groups to discuss *Talking points: What is a poem?* and to come to an agreement about what a poem is (or is not), then to share their definition of a poem in a class discussion.

Talking points: What is a poem?

A poem has a shape to it.

A poem is a number of verses which rhyme.

A poem has to have a rhythm.

It can be anything from a single thought to a long narrative.

You know it is a poem because of the way the words are set out on the page.

A poem does not follow any rules.

A poem can be about anything at all.

Poems are meant to be spoken.

Poetry was written in the past – not now.

A poem is a piece of writing that uses words chosen for their sound and suggestive power as well as their sense.

A poem is any group of words set out in a pattern that is different from prose.

Responding to poetry
It is important to help children enjoy and value their own response to a poem. A poem may be open-ended with a number of different interpretations possible. But because of the way comprehension is tested, children often think that a poem has a single interpretation. This activity is designed to help them to understand that a poem may be interpreted in a number of ways and that different interpretations may be valid.

Give the children the poem 'Sitting in the doorway'. Ask them individually to study the poem and to picture for themselves who is sitting in the doorway and what the doorway is like. You might want to ask such questions as: Is this a man or woman? A boy or a girl? Old or young? What are they wearing? What sort of building does the doorway belong to? What does it look like? What about the weather, time of year, time of day? Who else is there?

Share ideas in groups and in a class discussion, to consider who is 'right'. Encourage the class to accept that there is no right answer; ask the children to imagine that they work as editors for a publisher and that the poem is to be included in a book. It is their job to talk to an illustrator to decide what they want the illustration to be like. Ask groups to draw and discuss their ideas for illustration, before sharing them with the whole class. Again you can make the point that there cannot be a single 'right' answer. Some children may suggest that they would not have an illustration at all. Invite them to give their reasons and discuss how not illustrating the poem leaves it to the readers to make their own interpretations of the poem, whereas an illustration may influence them to interpret the poem in a particular way. Look at illustrations of the same poem by different illustrators, and discuss reasons for difference and the children's preferences.

Talk about poems generally, and their feature of being open to interpretation and comment. Look at single words or phrases and consider why they are ambiguous, and how the poet is making use of this feature of language.

> **Sitting in the doorway**
>
> Sitting in the doorway
> With nothing to eat,
> Feeling the cold
> Biting my feet.
>
> Sitting in the doorway
> With nothing to do,
> At the back of the line —
> The end of the queue.
> Sitting in the doorway
> With nowhere to hide
> From the night's bitter chill
> And the hunger inside.
>
> Sitting in the doorway
> With nothing.
>
> *John Foster*

Discussing poems

Teaching children some key technical vocabulary can enable them to discuss poetry more effectively. Some key features of poems are rhyme, rhythm, imagery, stanza and names of different forms of poetry. Children should learn to recognise how authors use a variety of techniques to expand the literal meaning of words, or use words to create an emotional response. In addition, their evaluation and understanding of a poem may depend on their knowledge of alliteration, assonance, onomatopoeia, imagery, symbolism, irony, metaphor and simile. It is important to model analysis and evaluation of poems, so that every child has experience of this, before asking children in their groups to provide an analysis. Teaching the children to recognise such features as a simile or a metaphor enables them to discuss what effect the simile or metaphor has.

I like this poem
Ask groups to choose a poem which they particularly like and to present it to the class, giving the reasons why they have chosen that

particular poem. Encourage them to elaborate on their reasons rather than simply saying, for example, 'Because it's funny.' Encourage them to think about how to make their presentations effective. For example, are there any points where they should pause? Are there any words or phrases that need to be emphasised, perhaps by raising or lowering their voice? Are there any gestures they could make to help bring the poem to life? What technical vocabulary will they use to explain their reasons for enjoying the poem?

Pairs of poems
Ask groups to choose two poems which are linked in some way, for example because they are on the same theme, use the same poetic form, are by the same poet, or are a complete contrast. Invite them to present their two poems and the reasoning behind their choices to the class.

A poetry programme
Ask groups to prepare a poetry programme for the radio on a theme or a particular poet. The theme can be related to the topic you are studying or alternatively you can set them a theme such as space, water, fire, weathers or spring. They could focus on a contemporary poet such as Michael Rosen, Allan Ahlberg, Roger Stevens, Julia Donaldson or Valerie Bloom; on a nineteenth-century poet such as Edward Lear or Christina Rossetti; or a twentieth-century poet such as Walter de la Mare or Charles Causley; or on the Children's Laureate.

After preparing together, each of the group should read and comment on a poem. Encourage them to choose an appropriate piece of music to play at the start and end of their programme. They can record their programmes and take it in turns to play them to the other members of the class. The class can evaluate presentations, pointing out strengths in relation to the talk Learning Intention of the session and suggesting ideas for development.

Performing poems
Varying your voice can really make a difference for the listener; it can help to change or create an atmosphere, to communicate

feelings, to portray a character or to convey the meaning of a poem. The activities in this section are designed to help children to understand how they can use the power, tone, pace and emphasis of their voice to provide variety in their performance.

Power
Explain that the words or lines in a poem can be spoken loudly and powerfully or softly and gently. They can be shouted, clipped, whispered or murmured.

Ask the children to study the poem 'Colour story – from gold to silver', thinking about how they can use the power of their voice differently when speaking different lines. Ask groups to rehearse taking a line each, in turns, to read the poem aloud, then to discuss how they used the power of their voices to read different lines.

Colour story – from gold to silver

Gold is a blaring trumpet call.
Blue is a shivering stream.
Yellow is a tickle of laughter.
White is the whistling dream.

Red is a scream, a strangled cry.
Orange is the spluttering flames.
Grey is the murmur of mist.
Silver is the rattle of chains.

John Foster

Tone
Talk about how you can use the tone of your voice to convey different feelings. For example, you can use a sharp tone to convey anger, a sneering tone to suggest dislike, a flat tone to suggest disappointment or a harsh tone to express disapproval.

Ask groups to prepare a performance of 'Overheard on a saltmarsh'. Encourage them to experiment by using a range of tones to say aloud what the goblin says – as if the goblin is angry, or pleading with the nymph, or frustrated or just bored. Also experiment with tone, saying what the nymph says – for example as if she is annoyed, as if she finds the goblin's request funny, or as if she feels offended. Ask them to decide which tone works best for the goblin and which works best for the nymph. Share their performances with the rest of the class and ask for positive feedback for performers.

> ### Overheard on a saltmarsh
>
> Nymph, nymph, what are your beads?
> Green glass, goblin. Why do you stare at them?
> Give them me.
>   No.
> Give them me. Give them me.
>   No.
> Then I will howl all night in the reeds,
> Lie in the mud and howl for them.
>
> Goblin, why do you love them so?
>
> They are better than stars or water,
> Better than voices of winds that sing,
> Better than any man's fair daughter,
> Your green glass beads on a silver ring.
> Hush I stole them out of the moon.
>
> Give me your beads, I desire them.
>   No.
> I will howl in a deep lagoon
> For your green glass beads. I love them so.
> Give them me. Give them me.
>   No.
>
>   Harold Monro

Pace
Talk about how you can vary the pace of a performance by speaking at different speeds. Ask the children in groups how they would vary the pace when performing the poem 'The eagle'. Prompt them to think about how the pace of their reading could be used to bring

out the contrast between the stillness of the first five lines and the movement in the last line.

Emphasis

Explain how to use power and tone of voice to emphasise particular words, phrases or lines. Ask the children which words and phrases they would want to stress in a reading of 'The eagle'. Then encourage them to prepare a presentation of the poem.

The eagle

He clasps the crag with crooked hands:
Close to the sun in lonely lands,
Ring'd with the azure world, he stands.

The wrinkled sea beneath him crawls;
He watches from his mountain walls,
And like a thunderbolt he falls.

Alfred, Lord Tennyson

Different voices

Discuss how the performance of a poem can often be made more interesting by using more than one voice. Using the poem 'November', display the list of words below and ask groups to think together to decide on two or three words which best sum up the feelings about November expressed in the poem.

miserable   exciting   dull   gloomy   boring   dreary   chilly
awful   hard   interesting   grim   beautiful   horrible
unpleasant   calm   mysterious   lively

Discuss what impression children would want a reading of the poem to create. Divide the class into five groups. Allocate two lines of the poem to each group. Ask them to prepare a reading of their part of the poem, deciding whether they will use one voice for a particular word and which words the whole group will speak. Produce and record a class reading of the poem; play the poem back so that the children can evaluate their oral performance.

Curriculum activities and games

> **November**
>
> November is a grey road
> Cloaked in mist.
> A twist of wood-smoke
> In the gathering gloom.
> A scurrying squirrel
> Hoarding acorns.
> A steel-grey river
> Glinting in the twilight.
> A grey rope
> Knotted around a threadbare tree.
>
> John Foster

Performing poems in groups
Ask groups to choose a poem to perform. Two poems are provided here as examples. If needed, you can provide a checklist for children to consider as they discuss their performance.

Checklist for poetry performance:

What ideas and feelings does the poem express?

What message or feeling do you want your reading to convey?

How will you divide up the poem? Will some parts be spoken by individuals or pairs? Which parts will be spoken by the whole group?

Are there particular words or phrases that you want to emphasise?

Does the poem rhyme? Are there any rhyming words you want to stress?

What tone of voice will you use? Will you vary the tone in particular parts?

Think about the poem's rhythm. Does it vary from verse to verse or have the same rhythm throughout?

Talk about stories, poems and drama

Will the pace of your reading be fast or slow?

Are there any actions or gestures you could make that will add to the performance?

From 'The brook'

I slip, I slide, I gloom, I glance,
Among my skimming swallows,
I make the netted sunbeams dance
Against my sandy shallows.

I murmur under moon and stars
In brambly wildernesses;
I linger by my shingly bars;
I loiter round my cresses.

And out again I curve and flow
To join the brimming river,
For men may come and men may go,
But I go on forever.

Alfred, Lord Tennyson

Past, present, future

Tell me, tell me, smiling child,
What the past is like to thee?
"An Autumn evening soft and mild
With a wind that sighs mournfully."

Tell me, what is the present hour?
"A green and flowery spray
Where a young bird sits gathering its power
To mount and fly away."

And what is the future, happy one?
"A sea beneath a cloudless sun;
A mighty, glorious, dazzling sea
Stretching into infinity."

Emily Brontë

Talking points for poems

In this section activities are designed to help children to look carefully at the stories and poems they read, to discuss and consider points about the text, and to articulate their ideas and the reasons for their ideas. Using the *Talking points* as a stimulus, children working in groups can negotiate a range of points of view and reach a group consensus to share with the class. Remind the children that it is essential to use exploratory talk when discussing talking points, and that aspects of their discussion will be brought out in the closing plenary. Thus the quality of their talk together is as crucial as its content.

Note that the *Talking points* given are provocative statements rather than questions. Statements support extended discussion without the pressure to find an answer. You can readily devise your own talking points for poems you wish your class to discuss. A further discussion activity is to ask groups to create talking points based on a poem. Collect these in and choose 10 or 12 points for a discussion session.

I was bullied once

I was bullied once
Now I'm a bully too.
They took it out on me.
So I'll take it out on you.

John Foster

Talking points: 'I was bullied once'

Talk together to share your ideas about the poem 'I was bullied once'.

Make sure that everyone is asked to say what they think, and why.

The 'I' in the story is talking about school.

By 'once' the writer means 'one time'.

'They' in this poem means a gang.

Talk about stories, poems and drama

'Took it out on' means that the bullies were angry about their own lives.
Everyone is bullied at some time.
Bullying means being hit.
Bullying is often meant to be a joke.
The writer is proud to be a bully now.
It is fair to take it out on others if you have been bullied yourself.
You can always find people who are easy to bully.
You have to get used to being bullied as part of growing up.
Someone should help the writer.

'The listeners' by Walter de la Mare

Provide groups with the text of 'The listeners' (openly available on the Internet) and with the *Talking points*. Ask children to discuss each statement, starting by saying whether they agree with it or not, and providing their reasons. Ask children to use evidence from the poem to support their views, and to discuss all ideas with respect, before coming to a group decision which they can share with the class.

Talking points: 'The listeners'

'The listeners' is a poem that is sinister and menacing.
The main point of the poem is the knocking on the door.
No one lives in the house any more.
The horse makes a lot of noise in this poem.
The traveller is a man and he is bossy.
He has got the wrong house.
The listeners are actually friendly, glowing things.
They can only exist when the moon shines.
The man frightens the listeners.
There are no listeners, only a man and a horse.

Curriculum activities and games

He did not keep his promise because he arrived too late.

The poem has only five sentences.

Silence cannot 'surge'.

The horse is not afraid at first, then gets scared and gallops off.

We are all listeners.

This poem is a mystery story.

The way through the woods

They shut the way through the woods
Seventy years ago.
Weather and rain have undone it again
And now you would never know
There was once a road through the woods
Before they planted the trees.
It is underneath the coppice and heath,
And the thin anemones.
Only the keeper sees
That, where the ring-dove broods
And the badgers roll at ease,
There was once a road through the woods.

Yet, if you enter the woods
Of a summer evening late,
Where the night-air cools on the trout-ringed pools,
Where the otter whistles his mate,
(They fear not men in the woods,
Because they see so few.)
You will hear the beat of a horse's feet,
And the swish of a skirt in the dew,
Steadily cantering through
The misty solitudes,
As though they perfectly knew
The old lost road through the woods...
But there is no road through the woods.

Rudyard Kipling

Talk about stories, poems and drama

> **Talking points: 'The way through the woods'**
>
> *You will see a ghost if you go in the woods.*
>
> *The road through the woods is still there.*
>
> *The animals are afraid to go near the road.*
>
> *The road was there before the woods.*
>
> *The woods are full of creatures that no one sees.*
>
> *It is easy to tell where the road was.*
>
> *Everywhere has changed completely since 70 years ago.*
>
> *The woods are quiet and lonely.*
>
> *People keep away from the woods.*
>
> *If you go there at night, you'll imagine what it used to be like.*

Talk and writing poems

Ways into writing poems can occupy an entire book! But briefly, this *Jumpstart!* book suggests ways to talk about poetry that help children think of poems as accessible, interesting and achievable. Any type of poem is more readily written if the child has had the chance to share stimulus ideas, and if they know that their first attempts at writing will be looked at and commented on with respect. It is quite usual for writers to work in this collaborative way, and children can gain confidence from knowing that their discussions follow in a terrific tradition of joint endeavour. Percy and Mary Shelley, the Bloomsbury Group, the Inklings, the Beatles – writers do well when they have the support and encouragement of others. To discuss ideas, then write individually, and go on to share writing and to talk again about what has been created is an effective model for getting things done.

Poets write because they have something to say, and if children can find their voice as a poet in your classroom you are offering them an invaluable means to express themselves. Some of them may carry on writing throughout their lives.

TALK ABOUT DRAMA AND IMPROVISATION

Drama activities provide children with the opportunity to explore situations and people's reactions to them in the same way that stories do. Through placing themselves imaginatively in various roles, children are able to understand how people think and feel in a range of circumstances.

Scenarios for groups or pairs
The activities in this section consist of scenarios for groups or pairs to act out. Having acted out a scenario, the children can then discuss how the characters felt and what prompted them to behave in particular ways.

Family matters
Encourage pairs to role play a scene in which a parent and child have an argument either because the child won't do as they are asked or because the parent won't let the child do something. Ask them to do the scene more than once, showing how it might end differently, depending on how the child and parent behave towards one another.

Invite pairs to role play an argument between two siblings because one of them has borrowed something from the other one without permission.

It's your fault!
Invite pairs to act out a scene in which brothers or sisters have broken or damaged something and are trying to blame each other for what has happened.

I'm so worried
Model how to sympathise, offer comfort, help someone to keep talking and give friendly counsel. Ask groups to role play a scene in which a young person confides in friends that her parents are going to separate and that she is worried because she thinks she must have done something to cause it. Also she doesn't know what's going to happen to her – Who is she going to live with, and will she have to move to another part of the country?

Talk about stories, poems and drama

The tattoo
Act out a scene in which an elder brother or sister tells their sibling that they're thinking of getting a tattoo. Their younger brother or sister tries to persuade them not to get one.

You promised!
Ask groups to role play a scene in which there is an argument between two friends because one of them has broken a promise to keep a secret. Encourage them to take it in turns to be the person who has broken the promise.

Under pressure
Ask groups to role play a scene in which a group of friends put pressure on someone to do something that the person does not want to do, such as go into a derelict house or to carry out a dare. Encourage them to take it in turns to be the person being pressurised. Which person resisted the pressure most effectively?

Invite pairs to act out a scene in which someone asks their friend to tell a lie to prevent them from getting into trouble.

Not guilty
Act out a scene in which someone is accused of something they did not do, for example stealing something or posting a hurtful message about someone. They can take it in turns to be the person who is accused and discuss how it feels.

The wallet
Ask the children in groups to imagine they are playing in the park when they find a wallet containing £50. Two of the children want to keep the money and share it between them. The others think they should hand it in. Act out the scene in which they argue about what they should do. You could ask some groups for destructive, angry argument, and others for constructive, exploratory argument. After watching the dramas, discuss the likelihood of each outcome happening and the consequences of each.

To tell or not to tell
Ask the children in pairs to imagine that they witnessed a person being bullied. One of them argues that they should report it. The other is frightened that the bullies will take it out on them if they report it. They discuss what they should do.

A better offer
Ask the children to imagine that two friends have made an arrangement to do something together at the weekend, such as to go into the town or to go for a bike ride. One of them then gets invited to do something they'd prefer to do, for example to go on a trip to an adventure playground. Act out the scene in which the person with the better offer discusses with an adult what they should do.

The odd one out
Ask groups to imagine they are a group of friends who are planning to pool their money and to go to the arcade to play the machines. One of them is against the idea because they think gambling is a mug's game. A heated argument ensues.

Planning a play script
Invite the children to work in a group and to plan a play script together. Explain that they will need to discuss and decide on a setting, as well as on the scenario and the characters.

They can either choose their own setting or you can suggest: a school classroom, a school playground, a fairground, a shopping precinct, a forest, a derelict house, a castle, a churchyard.

Encourage them to discuss what the focus of the play will be. What will happen in it? Will it convey a message to the audience, for example about the consequences of behaving in a particular way? They can either develop their own scenario or choose one from this list: an accident, a quarrel, a discovery, a dare, a crisis, a crime, a quest, a natural disaster, something lost or found.

Explain that they will need to decide who the main characters are going to be and what type of person each one is. Who the characters are will depend on the scenario they have chosen. Encourage them to make a list of the main characters and to discuss what sort of people they are. For example, they may be a group of three friends, one of whom is the leader of the group, one of whom always does what the leader suggests and one of whom is prepared to challenge the leader's suggestions.

Encourage the children to take on the roles of their characters and to improvise each scene of their play before drafting their script.

CHAPTER 8
Summary and resources

Our daughter began her Year 12 English studies at school and by half term was doing very well indeed. However, at Parents' Evening we were surprised that her teachers were rather less than pleased with her. They were dismayed and frustrated by her attitude to group work. 'She is an excellent student; but always refuses to join in discussion groups, and will not contribute orally in class,' they told us. 'She will never say a word.'

Since both of us are advocates of the importance of speaking and listening in education, and our daughter seemed to be articulate and willing to talk to her friends, family and a range of others, this came as something of a shock. We went home and asked her why she was not willing to discuss her ideas in school. 'Well,' she said, 'they've been telling me to stop talking in class for the last ten years, so I'm not going to start now!'

Lyn Dawes and Neil Mercer

THE IMPORTANCE OF TALK

Our dilemma, as teachers, is that asking for quiet is part of the work that we do on behalf of every child; but unless children express their ideas aloud, those ideas may never fully develop. Children asked not to speak may never really understand why. They may harbour misconceptions; they may never use important new vocabulary aloud; and they may feel that whatever they say is somehow not good enough.

In this *Jumpstart!* book we suggest that an effective way to resolve this dilemma is to teach children the skills that will allow them to

Summary and resources

talk in class, not in an informal and chatty manner, but in ways that enable themselves and their classmates to learn. Some lessons, ideas and concepts need quiet concentration. Some benefit from discussion. There must be time for both conditions. We teachers can easily organise both quietness and collaborative talk.

In order to discuss their ideas, children need lessons in:

1   awareness of the importance of talk for learning;
2   skills such as listening, reasoning, explaining and negotiating;
3   understanding and using suitable 'ground rules' for talking together in a group.

In addition, children need activities which will give them the chance to use their developing talk skills in a range of contexts, with carefully considered Learning Intentions and chances to evaluate talk in Plenary Discussions. Luckily the National Curriculum provides endless useful contexts for helping children to develop into articulate, listening youngsters. The National Curriculum also states very clearly that spoken language skills should be taught and learned in classrooms. All this is very heartening for teachers as they work towards helping children to develop their discussion skills.

Jumpstart! Talk for Learning provides games, activities and scenarios for you to use and consider. These suggestions can also be the starting points or examples from which you develop your own activities to suit your class. They can be adapted to their particular needs, and the topics you are covering. For example, it is straightforward to create your own sets of talking points when you want to focus discussion around a concept, artefact, story or mathematical idea.

With all the pressures to teach writing and reading skills, it is difficult sometimes to keep a focus on talk. We suggest you have regular days, sessions or activities organised, such as 'No Pens Day Wednesday' (see the resources that follow), and give yourself and the children the chance to evaluate their effectiveness.

Evaluation of learning is something we teachers do all day every day. Talk provides the opportunity to hear what children think about curriculum areas. You can evaluate both the child's competence in a subject and their capacity to use talk skills. You can use talk to help children better to understand the complexities of written evaluation, an important skill. Children taught how to use exploratory talk are proud of their talk skills, and you will find that they will use talk more effectively in the playground or other settings.

In summary, our aim is that children in your class will leave you at the end of the year knowing that both you and their classmates are interested in what they think. We envisage children spending ten years in school being encouraged to express their ideas, and developing their understanding of how to hear and accommodate a range of points of view – so that at any stage from Year 2 to Year 12 they will want to talk about the lessons you offer them, and are fully able to take part in the sort of classroom discussions that will lead to reflection and deeper learning.

Lyn Dawes and John Foster

OTHER RESOURCES

The Communication Trust
The Trust's *No Pens Day Wednesday* encourages schools to put down their pens and to run a day of speaking and listening activities. The Trust provides everything to run the day, which you can download for free from www.thecommunicationtrust.org.uk/projects/no-pens-day-wednesday/.

The Trust also provides some useful resources for assessing the progress of children's skills in using talk: www.thecommunicationtrust.org.uk/resources/resources/.

Thinking Together
Based at the University of Cambridge, this project is a dialogue-based approach to the development of children's thinking and learning:

Spoken language enables us to do much more than share information - it enables us to think together. But as teachers, do we always use it to best advantage? And do we give enough attention to enabling children to use language as a tool for learning and problem-solving?

On this website we explain how years of practical, classroom-based research in several countries and with learners of all ages has provided useful answers to these questions. We also provide some downloadable material for researchers and teachers, with links to useful books, research projects and other websites.
https://thinkingtogether.educ.cam.ac.uk/resources/

National Teaching Fellowship Scheme
Web pages with a useful overview of theories of learning: www.learningandteaching.info/.

Scribd Inc.
Essay scaffold for the importance of drama in primary education, including social and academic advantages: www.scribd.com/doc/18042787/The-Importance-of-Drama-in-Primary-Education #scribd.

Children's Laureate
The position of Children's Laureate is awarded once every two years to an eminent writer or illustrator of children's books to celebrate outstanding achievement in their field. The Children's Laureate inspires by visiting schools: www.childrenslaureate.org.uk/.

Storytelling Day
A website celebrating the art of story-telling. For every child, story-telling is a beginning to literature and vocabulary use. Listening to and telling stories can help children to enjoy thinking about their lives and the lives of others, and to reflect on moral principles and values. Children can appreciate the importance of the story-teller, and take on this role themselves. They can experience ways that people from diverse backgrounds are brought together by stories.

It is important that children realise that creating stories does not require writing skills.

www.storytellingday.net/oral-traditions-storytelling-explored.html

Poetry by John Foster
From John's home page:

> Welcome to my website whoever you may be,
> Where you can browse and find out more about my poems and me.
> You can read about the books I've written and what I like to do.
> You can delve into my secrets, try to write a poem or two.
> Let the menu be your guide, where you go is up to you.
> www.johnfosterchildrenspoet.co.uk/index.php/my-poems

Talking points: Discussion activities in the primary classroom by Lyn Dawes
The book provides an introduction on how to help children learn the skills of group discussion, offering six essential Talk Lessons to use in the classroom, alongside suggestions on how teachers can plan their lessons with a talk focus, set learning outcomes and create their own talking points to suit topics they are teaching: www.routledge.com/books/details/9780415614597/.

Language for Learning Group, Bradford: *Talking Children*
A successful talk-focused approach to teaching and learning in primary education, including a comic to take home and discuss with parents: https://bso.bradford.gov.uk/news/10730-the-talking-children-comic.

National Literacy Trust: *Words for Life*
Terrific resources for teachers: www.literacytrust.org.uk/.

The Children's Poetry Archive
Includes recordings of leading contemporary children's poets such as Michael Rosen, Brian Patten and Valerie Bloom: www.childrenspoetryarchive.org.

The Poetry Zone
A website run by the poet Roger Stevens. Its aim is to give children a chance to publish their poems and to share their views on the poetry they read. Children can upload their poems, comment on other people's poems, submit reviews on recent collections and enter poetry competitions. There are interviews with a number of children's poets and there is a teacher's section where you can share ideas for teaching poetry: www.poetryzone.co.uk.

Poems to perform
Two anthologies of poems which are particularly useful as they offer poems which children can perform:

1 *Poems to Perform: A classic collection chosen by the Children's Laureate*, ed. Julia Donaldson (Macmillan, 2014)
2 *I've Got a Poem for You: Poems to perform*, ed. John Foster (Oxford University Press, 2010)

Jumpstart! PSHE by John Foster
This book provides a wide range of talk activities for PSHE lessons encouraging children to share their views on issues that concern them, such as bullying, to explore social issues, such as prejudice and discrimination and to learn to think for themselves and to make their own decisions: www.routledge.com/9781138892217.

Get ready to...

Jumpstart!

The *Jumpstart!* books contain 'quick-figure' ideas that could be used as warm-ups and starters as well as possibly extended into lessons. There are more than 50 games and activities for Key Stage 1 or 2 classrooms that are practical, easy-to-do and vastly entertaining.

To find out more about other books in the Jumpstart! series, or to order online, please visit:

www.routledge.com/u/jumpstart/

Routledge
Taylor & Francis Group

David Fulton Books

www.routledge.com/teachers

Printed in Great
Britain
by Amazon